LITE...

Fowey, the 'Troy Town' of 'Q'

FOR ITS SIZE, Cornwall c
literary heritage than any oth
There are thousands of wo
born authors and those wh
they saw and stayed, the
county being right for their
paused here a while. This
likewise profoundly influen
tors, craftsmen and compos
This small book shows how
phere and character of the
its legends and its people
aspects of literature. It is
landscape described in no
autobiographies, poems, o
guidebooks and other to
There are also the places

lived or visited. The reader will find pleasure in the sense of discovery when relating authors' descriptions to actual places in the Cornish scene.

It is impossible to comment upon every writer in a book of this size, so a personal selection is taken from those who have penned works of, on, or about the county, or have some other connection. They range from the lesser-known to the literary giants who have all used the landscape to enrich the literary heritage of Cornwall. The gazetteer narrows the choice by the use of districts which have attracted a concentration of writers. Indeed, some places seem the private realm of their authors, such as Fowey and its intimacy with Sir Arthur Quiller-Couch ('Q') and Daphne du Maurier.

knowledge that it is 'Cornwall'. It can avoid the need to be strictly accurate and allows the author to select the best of Cornwall. Some novels, however, are set so casually in Cornwall that they could be anywhere, their authors deliberately using 'Cornish' names solely to bring an element of romance!

Cornish legends and folklore are a rich source for writers with imagination, but the activities of the people also provide good material. Probably the two most important influences are the romance of the Cornish tin and copper mining industry, with its hardships, danger and potential wealth, and the sea, with all its aspects of fishing, seafaring, shipwrecks and smuggling. Above all, there is a certain spirit that sets Cornwall apart from any other place.

THE SPIRIT OF CORNWALL

The very fabric of this westering Atlantic peninsula — its rocks, cliffs and the sea — is the spirit of Cornwall, that immeasurable thing which has inspired many authors and artists in their work. This is nowhere better expressed than in Denys Val Baker's *The Spirit of Cornwall* and *The Timeless Land*. D. M. Thomas follows the theme in many of his own and fellow poets' works in his collection *The Granite Kingdom* (another well-chosen title). The ever-present granite and slate which give such permanence to the landscape often surface in Sir John Betjeman's Cornish poems and prose.

While Betjeman's north Cornwall is wild, the granite West Penwith is more mysterious and primeval with its great shaped boulders and relics of the ancients. The spirit is most strongly felt here in the far west; the landscape is brooding but never still, always a wind and the sea crawling far below. "Walk here in the twilight of a wintry afternoon," wrote Ruth Manning-Sanders of Land's End, "when nothing is to be seen but the huge dim shapes of the silently withdrawing cliffs ... It is then that the sense of the primordial, the strange and savage, the unknown, the *very long ago*, fills the dusk with something that is akin to dread. It is then that the place becomes haunted: a giant heaves grey limbs from his granite bed..."

W. H. Hudson gave a memorable account of a winter storm across Zennor Hill. "Now it seemed to me, out there in spirit on the hill, that the darkest imaginings of men...was not so dark

Rocks around Zennor. "...the huge granite boulders bulging out of the earth like presences." (D.H. Lawrence, *Kangaroo*)

as this dreadful unintelligible and unintelligent power that made us, in which we live and move and have our being." While Hudson was exhilarated by the wildness of this magical Zennor area, the poet John Heath-Stubbs seems to have found no quiet here, writing of a "wicked country sloping to hateful sunsets." But the granite moors are not all menace, for D.H. Lawrence was at peace at Zennor and Virginia Woolf loved it too. Bodmin Moor is another granite district which shares this timeless quality, expressed in the writings of Daphne du Maurier and others. The presence of the granite moors can be uplifting, and the poet John Harris wrote of Carn Brea:

What joy to taste the stillness of the moors!
I feel afraid to shake their holiness
By breathing freely.

THE CORNISH LANGUAGE AND LITERATURE

A special aspect of Cornwall's heritage is its own language. Despite the advance of English, Cornish was still widely spoken in 1542 when Andrew Borde wrote: "In Cornwall is two speeches, one is naughty Englysshe and the other is Cornysshe speche. And there be many men and women the which cannot speake one word of Englysshe, but all Cornysshe." Later that century, John Norden wrote that the Cornish tongue was corrupted but easier to pronounce than Welsh, "for they strayne not their

wordes so tediouslye throwgh the throate, and so harshlye throwgh and from the Roofe of the mouth." The gentry and the people had lately begun to use English, although Cornish was still common to the west of Truro.

The last acclaimed Cornish speaker was the Mousehole fishwife Dolly Pentreath, who died in 1777 — her age variously stated between 91 and 102! The lawyer, antiquarian and naturalist Daines Barrington met her in 1768, although other women were said to be speaking Cornish together at that time. Dolly Pentreath's granite memorial at Paul was erected in 1860 by Prince Louis Lucien Bonaparte, a nephew of Napoleon who was born and lived in England where he studied old languages and naturally took an interest in Cornish. However, the language in West Cornwall did not die out entirely with Dolly, as a memorial slate outside Zennor church names John Davey of Boswednack (died 1891) as the last to speak Cornish.

Literature in the Cornish language mainly survives in the Miracle Plays which include *The Ordinalia*, three plays perhaps of the late fourteenth century, the *Beunans Meriasek* ('The Life of St Meriasek') of 1504, and *Gwreans an Bys* ('The Creation of the World') of 1611. Such lengthy plays (of up to three days) would be performed in the open air at a playing place or Plain an Gwarry. The best known of these earthworks are at St Just-in-Penwith and St Piran's Round near Perranporth.

Cornish literature declined after the Reformation, due more to a sparcity of writers rather than the spread of English. The language is not quite dead, for the Cornish Gorsedd has revived Cornish studies, literature and language. Its driving force was Henry Jenner of St Columb, who wrote the *Handbook of the Cornish Language*. He was aided by Robert Morton Nance, whose *Cornish-English Dictionary* standardised spelling in 1938, although this was not the end of the debate. Another helper was A. S. D. Smith, who translated the Tristan legend into Cornish verse: *Trystan hag Isolt*. Today, perhaps more people can read, write and speak the Cornish language than in the past two cen-

turies. Knowledge of the language is seen as a very real means of restoring identity and pride in being Cornish.

The first Gorseth Kernow was held in the stone circle at Boscawen Un on 21 September 1928, when the Archdruid Pedrog of Wales installed Jenner as the first Grand Bard of Cornwall. Other bards initiated included literary men such as Nance, Sir Arthur Quiller-Couch, A. K. Hamilton Jenkin, Rev Canon Thomas Taylor, Charles Henderson, and the poet John Dryden Hosken. The Gorsedd is an annual event, when bards are admitted for their works in the arts, literature or other fields deemed to have benefitted Cornwall. Knowledge of the language and literary competitions are a part, helped by the establishment of the Cornish Language Board in the 1960s.

Dolly Pentreath's memorial at Paul churchyard. "...the last person who conversed in the ancient Cornish the peculiar language of this county..."

PLACE NAMES: THE LITERATURE OF THE MAP

Cornwall's name (Kernow in Cornish) may come from the Cornovii, meaning the 'horn people' who dwelt in this peninsula or horn of Britain. Cornubia is a Latinised version. The final form comes from the Saxon Cornwalas, 'the strangers of Corneu,' an indication of the perceived remoteness of the district. The further west one travels from the Tamar border, increasing elements of the Cornish language survive in place-names describing rivers, hills, rocks, cliffs, forts or other landscape features. A selection of these poetic-sounding names

picked at random might include Baldhu, Breage, Castle-an-Dinas, De Lank, Gwennap, Linkinhorne, Luxulyan, Nancledra, Polkanuggo, Trencrom, Woon Gumpas and Zennor. The common prefixes of Car-, Lan-, Pen-, Pol-, Ros- and Tre- are also found in surnames, as Hawker reminds us in the famous refrain from 'Sir Bevill — The Gate Song of Stowe': "Ay! by Tre, Pol and Pen, ye shall know Cornishmen..." Church dedications to Cornish saints provide an army of wonderful names too.

CORNWALL IN ANCIENT LITERATURE

The Greek sailor Pytheas noted the Cornish peninsula in about 330 BC, while two hundred years later, Diodorus Siculus wrote: "The inhabitants of that extremity of Britain called Belerion [West Penwith] both excel in hospitality, and also, from their intercourse with foreign merchants, are civilised in their manner of life." He described tin-streaming and smelting, the tin ingots being taken at low tide to the island 'Ictis' where merchants carried them off to Gaul and overland to the mouth of the Rhone. Ictis is probably St Michael's Mount, although there are other contenders along the south coast. Of passing interest are Cornwall's Dark Age memorial stones, inscribed with dedications in de-based Latin. The Slaughter and Tristan stones have other literary connections, described below.

St Michael's Mount, the ancient 'Ictis'.

CORNWALL, THE LAND OF LEGEND

Cornwall is rich in folklore, legends and tales of giants. Many were published in William Bottrell's *Traditions and Hearthside Stories of West Cornwall* (1870), and Robert Hunt's *Popular Romances of the West of England* (1865). Devonport-born Hunt was better known for his mining literature, the creation of the Miners Association of Cornwall and Devonshire and his work as Keeper of the Mining Record Office.

Large and strange granite rocks were frequently associated with legends and folklore. J. O. Halliwell called the Land's End district 'anciently the chosen land of the Giants,' and Hunt made much of those who lived among these western summits. The greatest was the Giant Bolster of St Agnes Beacon, who could step across the 6 miles (9.6km) to Carn Brea. The caricaturist George Cruikshank illustrated this for his friend Hunt's book, estimating Bolster to have been 12 miles (19.2km) high. Hilltops or crags with giants include Carn Brea, Carn Galver, St Michael's Mount, Trencrom (Trecrobben), and Treryn Dinas. Individual rocks have names such as the Giant's Bowl, Castle, Chair, Cradle, Crocks and Kettles, Dinner-Plate, Hand, Head, and Spoon. Large prehistoric monuments were often named Giant's Quoits.

Apart from giants, haunted Cornwall includes the Spriggans who guard treasure amongst

The Giant Bolster striding from the Beacon to Carn Brea a distance of six miles

Cruikshank's Giant Bolster strides between St Agnes Beacon and Carn Brea rocky tors and burial chambers, while the Buccas or Knockers can lead miners to a 'kindly lode' underground if treated with respect. Modern ghost stories include collections by Denys Val Baker and Mary Williams. The latter's *The Dark Land* (1975), set in the ancient landscape of west Cornwall, has a feeling of menace from its silent valleys and brooding moors closing in at dusk. *Ravenscarne* (1990) is a more recent work. Ruth Manning-Sanders wrote of giants, witches and the like, not in a Cornish context but undoubtedly influenced by her surroundings at Sennen.

Along the far north Cornish coast persists the legend of Cruel Coppinger, the strange pirate, smuggler and wrecker, of whom R. S. Hawker wrote. On a kinder note, the Cornish Saints have their own fascinating legends. Some are found in the Rev Sabine Baring-Gould's *Lives of the Saints*, although more information is provided by Canon G. H. Doble's *Cornish Saints Series*.

ARTHUR, TRISTAN AND LYONESSE

The greatest legends immortalised in literature are those of King Arthur, Tristan and Lyonesse. King Arthur's claim to Cornwall stems from the 1130s, when Geoffrey of Monmouth wrote *The History of the Kings of Britain*. He had Arthur born at Tintagel Castle, the son of Ygerna (Duchess of Cornwall) and Uther Pendragon (King of Britain). However, the real Arthur was defending Britain far from Cornwall back in the early sixth century, while Tintagel Castle is medieval. Perhaps old memories lingered when Geoffrey chose this site, as excavations have shown its importance in Arthurian times.

There are other places associated with Arthur on the wilds of Bodmin Moor, such as King Arthur's Bed, a natural rock-basin on Trewortha Tor, or King Arthur's Hall, a prehistoric earthwork on King Arthur's Downs. The Slaughter Stone by the River Camel (Geoffrey's 'Camblan') at Slaughterbridge is also King Arthur's Tomb, marking his grave or the scene of his last battle. Arthur is lucky to have a second grave at Warbstow Burrow. His sword Excalibur is claimed in legend by Dozmary Pool and Loe Pool. The latter tallies with the scene where "on one side lay the Ocean, and on one lay a great water..." in Tennyson's 'The Passing of Arthur'. Tennyson placed Arthur and his knights in the medieval age of chivalry, and chose Cornish locations from Tintagel to Lyonesse. Robert Hunt included some Arthurian legends in his *Popular Romances*.

The legendary Lyonesse or 'Lethowsow' lay between Land's End and the Isles of Scilly. This rich and fertile land and its 140 churches were

Thomas Hardy's drawing of Tintagel Castle. (*The Famous Tragedy of the Queen of Cornwall*, 1923)

overwhelmed by the sea, leaving the Sevenstones reef and the Scillies as remnants. Legend has it that one Trevillian escaped by swimming on horseback to the mainland. Tennyson's Arthur chased Mordred "back to the sunset bound of Lyonesse" until "the pursuer could pursue no more..." and then on a day

"when the great light of heaven
Burn'd at his lowest in the rolling year,
On the waste sand by the waste sea they closed.
Nor ever yet had Arthur fought a fight
like this last, dim, weird battle of the west."

Lyonesse is also associated with one of the greatest of all love stories, that of Tristan and Isolde (also Tristram and Isolt, Iseult or Essylt). These two tragic lovers were bound together by a magic love-potion, with unfortunate consequences since Isolde was Mark's queen and Tristan his nephew (or son in some versions).

The story is set in Cornwall and Brittany, and possibly based in part on truth. It may have originated in Cornwall in the sixth century, but the earliest surviving version is Béroul's *Le Roman de Tristan* from the early twelfth century. The best later version is the *Tristan* of Gottfried von Strassburg, a thirteenth century German poet. The legend was brought up to date by 'Q' in his last novel *Castle Dor*.

Coincidences in Cornwall's place-names and archaeology have lent support to the legend, placing it in the Fowey area. The iron-age fort at Castle Dore near Fowey was once believed to have become the palace of Mark, a known Cornish king of the mid-sixth century. Nearby Lantyan can be identified with Béroul's palace of Mark at 'Lancien'. Another connection is St Sampson's church at Golant, on the old Saint's Way from Padstow to Fowey. The Tristan Stone once stood by Castle Dore, but is now nearer Fowey. Its inscription reads: 'Drustaus-/Drustanus hic iacit Cunomori filius' or 'Here lies Drustanus [Tristan], son of Cunomorus [Mark]', the coincidence being almost too good to be true. Place-names further afield also tie in with the literature. Malpas, a crossing place at the

meeting of the Truro and Tresillian rivers, is said to be the scene of Isolde's trial, while the lovers' hiding place in the woods of 'Morrosi' could be Moresk further upstream at Truro. The 'Blanche Lande' or 'White Moor' might be the Hensbarrow china clay district.

In Tennyson's 'The Last Tournament', Tristram rode "toward Lyonesse and the west./Before him fled the face of Queen Isolt..." Matthew Arnold's poem 'Tristram and Iseult' described "The peerless hunter, harper, knight — Tristram of Lyoness," and Iseult left Ireland at her father's will,

"For the surge-beat Cornish strand,
Where the prince whom she must wed
Dwells on proud Tyntagel's hill,
Fast beside the sounding sea."

So, Arnold placed Mark's palace at Tintagel. A. C. Swinburne's 'Tristram of Lyonesse' described Tintagel, as did Thomas Hardy's play *The Famous Tragedy of the Queen of Cornwall*. Hardy also used the name Lyonesse for Cornwall in the love poem 'When I Set Out for Lyonesse', and for those who know Cornwall, it is hardly surprising he "came back from Lyonesse with magic in my eyes!"

TOPOGRAPHERS AND COUNTY HISTORIANS

Cornwall, so instantly recognised by its unique shape, was among the earliest counties to receive the detailed attention of map-makers and topographers. John Norden surveyed Cornwall in about 1584, but his *Topographical and Historical Description of Cornwall* (with maps of each county 'hundred') was not printed until after his death. Richard Carew's *Survey of Cornwall* (1602) provides a classic account of his native county.

Of more specialist interest, Dr William Borlase published one of the great early county archaeologies, *The Antiquities of Cornwall* in 1754. *The Natural History of Cornwall* followed in 1758. He was born at Pendeen Manor and was rector of Ludgvan for forty years. The Redruth surgeon William Pryce, published *Mineralogia Cornubiensis* in 1778, describing the working methods of Cornish tin and copper mines, and a standard work for mining historians.

The nineteenth century saw the publication of large county histories, often in several parts. The first volume of Richard Polwhele's *The History of Cornwall* appeared in 1803, and his work was followed by C. S. Gilbert's *An Historical Survey of the County of Cornwall* (1817-20), and F. Hitchins and S. Drew's *The History of Cornwall* (1824). Davies Gilbert published *The Parochial History of Cornwall* in 1838, "founded on the manuscript histories of Mr Hals and Mr Tonkin." Much later, Joseph Polsue's *A Complete Parochial History of the County of Cornwall* was published by William Lake in four volumes in 1867-72. In addition, G. C. Boase and W. P. Courteney's *Bibliotheca Cornubiensis* (1874-82) lists the publications of Cornish writers, and its three volumes indicate the importance of this work. Boase's *Collectanea Cornubiensa* is the county's own national biography up to 1890.

BOOKS OF CORNWALL

Countless books have been written on or about Cornwall. Among the authors of the nineteenth century was the eccentric Robert Stephen Hawker, vicar of Morwenstow in 1834-75. He was a writer and poet of some note, and his Cornish works include the entertaining *Footprints of Former Men in Far Cornwall* (1870). The Rev Sabine Baring-Gould, rector at Lewtrenchard in west Devon, wrote on many subjects including Cornwall and its antiquities. *A Book of Cornwall* (1899) was one of a larger regional series he wrote, and is mainly historical. Other books include *Cornish Characters and Strange Events* and *The Vicar of Morwenstow*, which recounts R.S. Hawker's life.

Some authors provided more detail on Cornish districts. The best include John Thomas Blight of Penzance, who wrote and illustrated the excellent *A Week at the Land's End* (1861) when still in his twenties, but sadly he spent his last forty years in the County Asylum at Bodmin. Blight's book is complemented by the Rev C. A. Johns's *A Week at the Lizard*, first published in the 1840s. Johns was also the author of *Flowers of the Field*.

An increasing number of more specialist books appeared in the twentieth century. Early natural history books include J.C. Tregarthen's *Wild Life at the Land's End* (1904) and *The Life Story of a Fox*, also set in the same district. *The Land's End* (1908) was the result of a winter stay at Zennor by William Henry Hudson, a noted author and naturalist with a special interest in birds. He first visited west Cornwall in 1905, and he fell for its charms immediately. He returned several times before his death in 1922, staying at Penzance and St. Ives.

In the 1930s, A. K. Hamilton Jenkin wrote *The Story of Cornwall*, and three detailed books which were later combined as *Cornwall and its People* (1945). He was born and lived at Redruth in the heart of the mining industry. His fame as a mining historian began in 1927 with *The Cornish Miner*. After years of research, his sixteen-volume *Mines and Miners of Cornwall* was published in 1961-70.

Geoffrey Grigson's *Freedom of the Parish* (1954) is a good account of Pelynt and its history, natural history and local industries. It is

Robert Stephen Hawker at his Vicarage door, Morwenstow.

mixed with some childhood memories, for he was born here where his father was the vicar. He also wrote *The Scilly Isles* (1948), and was general editor of the *About Britain Guides* for the 1951 Festival of Britain, writing the *West Country* and *Wessex* parts.

Mid-Cornwall has contributed a number of writers. A.L. Rowse was born at St Austell where he was educated before going up to Oxford University. A biographer and Tudor historian, his many Cornish-related books include *Tudor Cornwall, The Cornish in America, A Cornish Anthology* and *Stories from Trenarren*. Two Padstow men have written of Cornwall. Claude Berry gave a personal view in *A Portrait of Cornwall* (1949). Donald R. Rawe, playwright and poet, revised Berry's book in 1984, and wrote his own *A Prospect of Cornwall* (1986). James Turner, who lived below Delabole and near Wadebridge, described the county in *The Stone Peninsula* (1975). In *Vanishing Cornwall* (1967), Daphne du Maurier wrote from near Fowey of her worries about the changing face of the Cornwall she loved. Somewhat earlier, Lady Vyvyan of Trelowarren on the Lizard wrote short impressions of Cornwall, first as C.C.Rogers in *Cornish Silhouettes* (1924) and later as C. C. Vyvyan in *Our Cornwall* (1948).

Denys Val Baker, a prolific writer of short stories and autobiographies, promoted Cornish literature by founding and editing *The Cornish Review* against all odds in 1949-52, then reviving a new series in 1966-74. His two books, *The Timeless Land* (1973) and *The Spirit of Cornwall* (1980) went a long way to explain the essence of Cornwall that moves and influences so many writers and artists.

GUIDE BOOKS

County guide books form a large branch of literature. Some are of a high standard, such as John Murray's *A Handbook for Travellers in Devon and Cornwall*, first published in the mid-nineteenth century, and containing recommended tours and descriptions which are still highly readable and informative. Later books, for example C. S. Ward and M. J. B. Baddeley's *Thorough Guide Series* and the Ward, Lock guides, give useful historical details.

Cornwall was described in George Meason's *The Official Illustrated Guide to the Great Western Railway*, and some seventy years later that same railway promoted its services by publishing S. P. B. Mais's well-written *Cornish Riviera* in 1928. The value of such period books is that they record a Cornwall which has now largely vanished. We look back with nostalgia to the old or imagined 'real' Cornwall of these guides, written in an age of innocence before the motor car robbed the county of its remoteness. However, while Cornwall was still largely untouched by the modern tourist industry, it is surprising to learn how early tourism was established.

Still a personal favourite is John Betjemen's *Cornwall: A Shell Guide* (1964), a full revision of an earlier volume of 1935. He brings a personal touch and, as in his other writings and poems, he often looks back to the Cornwall he so loved in earlier years. Many of the book's photographs are by John Piper, with whom Betjeman was joint editor of the series.

The twentieth century has seen a proliferation of guides of all kinds — county books and local guides — all finding a ready sale among increasing numbers of visitors. While standards may vary, Cornwall has deservedly more than its fair share of such literature.

TRAVELLERS AND DIARISTS

Cornwall was included in tours around Britain by early writers, such as William Camden and John Leland. It has subsequently been described in numerous diaries, journals and travellers' accounts. The perseverance shown by many of these early 'tourists' puts the modern car-bound visitor to shame.

In the 1690s, Celia Fiennes took the south coast route through Cornwall from Millbrook and "passed over many very steep stony hills" to Looe. Beyond, she gave her famous description of Cornish road conditions, when she met "a deeper clay road, which the raine the night before had made it very dirty and full of water ... here my horse was quite down in one of these holes full of water." In 1724, Daniel Defoe

The Botallack Mine, visited by Wilkie Collins and other Victorians

described Cornwall in *A Tour Through the Whole Island of Great Britain*. He crossed the Tamar by ferry from Plymouth to Saltash, thence to Liskeard and down through the county to Land's End, where "being resolved to see the very Extremity of it, I set my Foot into the Sea, as it were, beyond the farthest Inch of dry Land West."

John Wesley's *Journals* illustrate his energy during many visits to Cornwall from 1743 to 1789. Although his chief concern was the salvation of the people, he did describe some places he visited and the difficulties of travelling on horseback over poor roads. For example, visiting Carn Brea and Land's End, crossing Bodmin Moor and preaching at his favourite Gwennap Pit.

An increasing number of visitors recorded their travels during the nineteenth century, and it would seem that few important figures in the literary world omitted to make at least one pilgrimage to Cornwall. As with Victorian guidebooks, the language of some of their descriptions makes amusing reading.

An early visitor was Baker Peter Smith, whose *Trip to the Far West* recorded a "pedestrious Excursion through various parts of Cornwall" in September 1839. Long before main-line railways, he entered Cornwall at Falmouth, having voyaged from London via Plymouth on the Dublin steamer *Royal Adelaide*. He walked 175 miles in seven days, ending at Launceston.

Exactly three years later, Charles Dickens celebrated his return from America by making an eight-day tour of Cornwall with John Forster (his biographer) and the artists Daniel Maclise and Clarkson Stanfield. They hired an open carriage and post-horses in Devon for their rapid journey down into Cornwall. There seems to have been much drinking, and they must have made a wild group. "I never laughed in my life as I did on this journey," Dickens wrote afterwards to C. C. Felton. Dickens looked after the money, Stanfield the maps, Forster the luggage, and Maclise, "having nothing particular to do, sang songs."

They descended several mines and visited St Michael's Mount, the Logan Rock and Land's

The Logan Rock. an early nineteenth century view.

End before turning for home. Forster, whose account lengthened the trip to nearly three weeks, added "Tintagel was visited, and no part of mountain or sea consecrated by the legends of Arthur was left unexplored." They were all awed by a sunset at Land's End, which Dickens later described in *A Christmas Carol*: "Down in the west the setting sun had left a streak of fiery red, which glared on the desolation for an instant, like a sullen eye, and frowning lower, lower, lower yet, was lost in the thick gloom of darkest night."

Dickens was hoping to find material in Cornwall for his new novel *Martin Chuzzlewit*, which he intended to open in a lighthouse or mine; instead the story began in a Wiltshire village "within an easy journey of the fair old town of Salisbury." He did not publish a diary of the Cornish trip, but he used elements of his experiences in short pieces in *Household Words* and *A Christmas Carol*.

Wilkie Collins was a close friend of Dickens and wrote many pieces for the latter's weekly periodicals. He is best known for the classic Victorian thriller *The Woman in White* and detective novel *The Moonstone*, but his Cornish connection comes from *Rambles Beyond Railways*, which described a walking tour made with his artist friend Henry Brandling in the summer of 1850. The title of course was very appropriate. The main line railway now reached Plymouth, but it was still nine years before Brunel's Royal Albert Bridge across the Tamar linked Cornwall directly to the rest of England. Collins did not intend to write a tourist guidebook, for he only described those places he cared to visit and was frank with his opinions of them too. These included Looe, Liskeard, the Cheesewring, the Lizard, Loe Pool, Logan Rock, Land's End, Tintagel and a descent of Botallack Mine. He also gave descriptions of the people, drama and legends.

Walter White (the Royal Society's Librarian) journeyed through the south of England into Cornwall, which he described in *A Londoner's Walk to the Land's End* (1855). He visited the usual spots in the far west, such as Carn Brea, St Ives and the Logan Rock. He was rather disappointed with Land's End and preferred not to descend the Botallack Mine.

Meanwhile, Alfred Lord Tennyson had toured Cornwall in May-July 1848, visiting Bude, Tinta-

gel, Polperro, the Logan Rock, Land's End, Lizard, Kynance Cove and St Ives: an itinerary worthy of a modern-day tourist. He returned in August-September 1860, visiting the old places and adding the Isles of Scilly, Falmouth, Truro and Perranporth. He aimed to walk at least ten miles a day whatever the weather. Much to Tennyson's annoyance, his wife had asked Francis Palgrave to keep an eye on him, and the trip was to end in an argument. For a time they were joined by the artists Holman Hunt and Val Prinsep and the poet-sculptor Thomas Woolner.

The Rev Francis Kilvert's diary of 19th July to 6th August 1870 gives a fascinating description of Cornwall during a stay with friends at Perranarworthal. He shows the efforts the Victorians took to reach places on daily excursions, often travelling by railway, horse vehicle and on foot. For example, for Land's End, they took trains to Truro and Penzance, a wagonette to Treen to visit the Logan Rock and on to Porthgwarra, from where the gentlemen walked along the cliffs to meet the ladies at their goal. A 50-mile round trip by horse carriage to the Lizard lasted from 8.30am to 11pm, while they returned from a trip to Gurnard's Head at 3am! Tintagel was a two-day affair, staying a night at the Royal Talbot at Lostwithiel and leaving early by waggonette and pair via Bodmin and Camelford. After visiting the castle, they left a little before 4pm to reach Lostwithiel in time to catch the Flying Dutchman train to Truro, but "alas, as Mrs. H[ockins] said quaintly, 'he flieth not below

THE LOGAN STONE, NEAR PENZANCE.

The Logan Rock, a Victorian view.

Plymouth', and we were a long time getting to our journey's end." (*Kilvert's Cornish Diary*, 1989)

Dinah Maria Mulock made a sixteen-day tour of Cornwall, visiting the Lizard, Land's End and 'King Arthur's Land,' which she recorded first in *The English Illustrated Magazine*, and then a book in 1884. Each instalment of this 'unsentimental journey through Cornwall' was illustrated by Charles Napier Hemy, the Falmouth-based artist. Mulock wrote under the name of Mrs Craik, her best known novel being *John Halifax, Gentleman*.

These earlier tours had the true adventure of an expedition, a sense now impossible when every part of Cornwall has been made accessible by improvements in road transport. Among the last of the old-style tours were those of C. Lewis Hind and A. G. Folliott-Stokes, made at the beginning of the new century. Lewis Hind gave a personal view in *Days in Cornwall*, mostly of walks made in 1907 with Charles Marriott to whom the book was dedicated. Hind sometimes travelled alone, such as a cycle ride across Bodmin Moor. In *The Cornish Coast and Moors* (c.1908), Folliott-Stokes related a coastal walk following coastguard paths from Marsland Mouth to Cremyll, with two excursions onto Bodmin Moor. This was long before the Cornwall Coastal Footpath became officially established.

A CHOICE OF WRITERS

There are writers Cornish-born and bred, while others have made Cornwall their home and source of inspiration. Many have woven the spirit of Cornwall into their novels or short stories. Writers with imagination have found a rich source in Cornwall's folklore and legends, while historical novelists have used the activities of the people, such as mining, the sea and in the Civil War period. Many writers are also poets. However, not all those living in Cornwall have necessarily written about the county. In more recent times such names include David Cornwell (John le Carré) and Colin Wilson. There is also Jessica Mann, whose crime books are set outside the county, although some elements of Cornwall ('Arthur's Castle') appear in her *Faith, Hope and Homicide* (1991). The Nobel Prize winner William Golding was born at St Columb Minor, returning to Cornwall later in life. Others — big names like D. H. Lawrence, Dylan Thomas or Virginia Woolf — have stayed in Cornwall briefly.

There are remoter Cornish connections. For example, Dr John Wolcot was educated in Cornwall and later practised in Truro for a few years until 1780, when he left for London to write satirical verse under the name of Peter Pindar. He took with him the St Agnes artist John Opie, whose portrait of him is in the County Museum and Art Gallery at Truro. The Brontë sisters' mother Maria and aunt Elizabeth were the daughters of Thomas Branwell, a merchant in Penzance. After Maria's early death, Elizabeth looked after the young children at Haworth in Yorkshire, no doubt telling them stories of Penzance and Cornwall. Daphne du Maurier described this Brontë connection in *Vanishing Cornwall*, comparing the moors of West Penwith and Haworth. The idea for *The Tale of Little Pig Robinson* is said to have come to Beatrix Potter when she saw a pig loaded onto a ship at Falmouth in 1894. She placed 'Stymouth' [Dartmouth?] in Devon, although the opening description of the busy fishing harbour is very like Newlyn.

THE VICTORIANS

The earlier novelists include Wilkie Collins, who used his observations in West Penwith for his novel *Basil* (1852), in which the coast between Porthgwarra and Logan Rock feature at the climax. *The Dead Secret* (1857) is less descriptive, but 'Porthgenna Tower' is in west Cornwall.

Charles Kingsley's *Westward Ho!* (1855) was partly written at Tonacombe near Morwenstow, so this part of north Cornwall (his 'Coombes of the Far West') and the Grenvilles of Stowe feature in the book. His later *Hereward the Wake* includes two visits by Hereward to Gweek on the Helford River.

R. M. Ballantyne, the author of *Coral Island*, collected material for *Deep Down: A Tale of the Cornish Mines* (1869) while living at Penzance. The story gives an informative account of Cornish mining at Botallack Mine near St Just. Around Penzance, he describes the Wherry Mine, fishing at Newlyn, and tin smelting, perhaps derived from a visit to the Chyandour works. Near Gurnard's Head, 'Wheal Dooem' deals with the practice of setting up fraudulent mining companies. Naturally, smuggling also comes into the story. In the same area, James Francis Cobb's *The Watchers on the Longships* (1876) concerns a period a hundred years before, and shows that the historical novel is not a feature of the twentieth century.

Thomas Hardy is associated with Wessex and Dorset, but his important Cornish connection is that he met his first wife Emma at St Juliot near Boscastle. He was sent there to make drawings and supervise the restoration of the church in 1870-2, and this part of his life forms the body of *A Pair of Blue Eyes* (1873), set at 'West Endelstow' near 'Castle Boterel'. Cornwall was his 'Off-Wessex' and in the short story *A Mere Interlude* (1885) he continued his habit of renaming towns, for example 'Pen-zephyr' (Penzance), 'Redrutin' (Redruth) or 'Trufal' (Truro).

An increasing number of Cornish novels appeared towards the end of the nineteenth century, many with a flavour of the sea. For example, Walter Besant's best book *Armorel of Lyonesse* (1890) is about the Isles of Scilly. Of Sabine Baring-Gould's many novels, *The Gaverocks* is set on the north coast near Padstow. His far better *In the Roar of the Sea* (1892) tells

Map of Thomas Hardy's Cornwall, or 'Off Wessex'

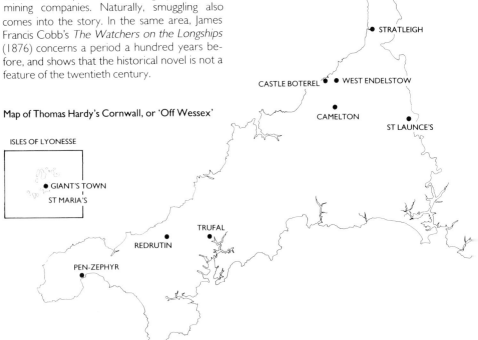

"A desperate struggle for life" in Botallack Mine
(R.M.Ballantyne, *Deep Down*)

of a young girl caught up in smuggling and wrecking around Pentireglaze — in many ways a forerunner of Daphne du Maurier's *Jamaica Inn*. Elizabeth Godfrey placed her *Cornish Diamonds* (1895) further along the north Cornish coast, at the Devon border. As in Hardy's book, there is a dramatic fall and rescue on a shaly cliff. Sir Arthur Quiller-Couch, who wrote under the pseudonym 'Q', was born in 1863 at Bodmin where his father was a doctor. His many novels and short stories include *Dead Man's Rock* (1887), *The Astonishing History of Troy Town* (1888), *The Splendid Spur* (1889), *The Delectable Duchy* (1893), *The Ship of Stars* (1899), and

From a Cornish Window (1906). He edited the short-lived *The Cornish Magazine*, in 1898-99. The 'Troy Town' of his stories is his beloved Fowey, where he lived from 1892 until his death in 1944. His grandfather was the naturalist Jonathan Couch of Polperro, whose notes were used by his son Thomas in the *History of Polperro*). 'Q' used him for 'Dr Unonius' in *Corporal Sam and Other Stories*, and the house at 'Polpier' was the home of a wartime naval reservist in *Nicky-Nan* (1915).

Joseph and Silas Hocking from Terras Moor near St Austell produced a huge number of popular Cornish novels around the turn of the century. Joseph said *The Spirit of the West* (1913) was "written within the sound of the Cornish sea and within sight of its glorious coastline ...There is no part of England more full of romance than Cornwall." He tried to make the spirit real in this story, and concluded that of his many Cornish stories of the last twenty-five years, "I am sure I have never got so near the heart of the Delectable Duchy." This last, once popular, expression belonged to 'Q', to whom it came while pacing the sands at St Ives one Easter.

The critic Sir Leslie Stephen owned Talland House at St Ives in 1881-96, where his family stayed for several months at a time, often playing host to literary friends. He is best known for editing the *Dictionary of National Biography*, but he was also a noted mountaineer (he edited *The Alpine Journal* in 1868-72), and is reported to have scrambled up a chimney "gangling and prehensile" at Gurnard's Head.

Sir Arthur Quiller-Couch ('Q') at The Haven, Fowey, in November 1943 six months before his death.
Cornish Studies Library

Right at the tail of the old century, and in the early years of the new, a number of writers converged on west Cornwall. Joseph Henry Pearce's *Inconsequent Lives* (1891) and *Ezekial's Sin: A Cornish Romance* (1898) were set around Mount's Bay, Newlyn and Lamorna ('Polurrian') Cove. Charles Lee caught Cornish life and especially the dialect in *The Widow Woman* (1897), set at 'Pendennack' or Newlyn, *Paul Carah Cornishman* (1898) at 'Porthvean' and *Dorinda's Birthday* (1911) at 'Porthmellan'. He also lived at Portloe, which is more obviously the 'Porthjulyan' of *Our Little Town* (1909).

Charles Marriott lived for a year from the autumn of 1901 at Lamorna and a further seven years at St Ives. His *The House on the Sands* (1903) was set across the bay at Gwithian. At this time, other authors associated with St Ives were C. Ranger Gull, A. G. Folliott-Stokes, and Mrs Havelock Ellis, author of *My Cornish Neighbours* (1906). Marriott knew Compton Mackenzie, who lived at Hayle, and also at Gunwalloe. Mackenzie's first novel *Carnival*

contains a Cornish background, but his much later and better known *Whisky Galore* was set far away on the Hebridean island of Barra. Marriott also knew Hugh Walpole, who lived a while in Truro, the 'Polchester' of his four books which began with *The Cathedral*.

During the Great War D. H. Lawrence and his German-born wife Frieda stayed in Cornwall, first at Porthcothan near Padstow from December 1915 before moving to Zennor in the following March. They stayed at the Tinners' Arms before renting a group of cottages at Higher Tregerthen. He completed *Women in Love* here, although it was not published until after the war. The Lawrences were looked upon with suspicion (not helped by the singing of German folk songs!) and the authorities gave them three days' notice to leave Cornwall in 1917. Lawrence had been content here and recorded the time through the eyes of Richard Somers in the chapter he called 'The Nightmare' in *Kangaroo* (1923). Of Zennor, he wrote: "It is a most beautiful place, a tiny village nestling under high, shaggy moorhills, a big

Zennor, a village and district much favoured in the early twentieth century

Godrevy Lighthouse "...it was a stark tower on a bare rock." (Virginia Woolf, *To the Lighthouse*)

sweep of lovely sea beyond, such lovely sea, lovelier than the Mediterranean... It is the best place I have been in."

Lawrence had hoped to found a writers' colony with Katherine Mansfield and the critic John Middleton Murry, with whom he had published the short-lived magazine *Signatures* in 1915. He called Higher Tregerthen their 'Rananim' and pursuaded them to come down in the spring of 1916, but it did not suit them. "It is not a really nice place. It is so full of stones..." wrote Mansfield, and they soon moved to a cottage in softer surroundings at Mylor near Falmouth. She was a writer of original and experimental stories, but was unwell and died of TB in 1923. Murry (whom she married in 1918) was a critic who edited the *Athenaeum* in 1919-23 and founded *The Adelphi* in 1923.

Sir Leslie Stephen's daughter Virginia Woolf spent her first childhood holidays at Talland House, St Ives, until her mother died in 1895 and the house was sold. This early Cornish experience made a great and lasting impact and her experimental novel *To the Lighthouse* (1927) used the house, view and St Ives Bay with the Godrevy lighthouse beyond, although she transferred the location to the Hebrides.

She returned in her writing and in person to Cornwall and the St Ives district in the 1920s — visits recorded briefly in her diaries.

Crosbie Garstin was born at Penzance in 1887, the son of Norman Garstin, a member of the Newlyn school of artists. After an adventurous life abroad, he settled back in Cornwall at Lamorna and St Buryan. Here in the 1920s he based his main Cornish work, the eighteenth-century Ortho Penhale trilogy of seafaring, smuggling and privateering: *The Owl's House*, *High Noon* and *The West Wind*. Garstin was also a poet and published his first collection *Vagabond Verses* in 1917. He drowned in a boating accident in 1930.

Kenneth Grahame's *Wind in the Willows* (1908), which originated from bedtime stories and letters to his son, contains several elements of Fowey. The Sea Rat, for example, gives a perfect description of Fowey when he encounters Ratty and Mole. Grahame met his friend 'Q' at Fowey in 1899, and was also married here.

Meanwhile, 'Q' continued his literary ouput unabated up until his death. In 1900 he edited the first *Oxford Book of English Verse*. He was knighted in 1910, and two years later became Professor of English Literature at Cambridge

University. He worked hard for the Cornwall Education Committee for thirty years, and during that time helped A.L. Rowse gain a scholarship to Oxford.

The name Daphne du Maurier also conjures up an immediate picture of Cornwall and Fowey. Her literary affair with the Fowey area, where she lived and set many of her novels, began in 1931 with *The Loving Spirit. Rebecca* brought her sudden acclaim in 1938, *The King's General* (1946) and *The House on the Strand* (1969) followed, and she completed *Castle Dor* (1962) for her friend 'Q' after his death. *Frenchman's Creek* (1941) is outside the district on the Helford estuary, but still with a nautical and historical flavour. *Jamaica Inn* (1936) is on Bodmin Moor.

Leo Walmsley lived in a small hut on Fowey harbour with his second wife in the early 1930s, and described his experiences in his semi-autobiographical *Love in the Sun* (1939). *Paradise Creek* (1963), an autobiography, records his return in the 1950s. Other books were set in Yorkshire, but *Angler's Moon* (1965) is again of Fowey, published the year before he died.

While Fowey is a major china clay shipping port, two novels by the poet Jack Clemo give good descriptions of the unique landscape where this important raw material is produced. *Wilding Graft* (1948) describes the area around St Stephen, while the fictitious clay village 'Carn Veor' is the centre of *The Shadowed Bed* (1986).

Howard Spring was born at Cardiff but lived at Mylor and then Falmouth from the 1940s until his death in 1965. This area around the Carrick Roads is in many of his novels, such as *My Son, My Son* (1938), *All the Day Long* (1959) and *Winds of the Day* (1964). *The Houses in Between* (1951) describes Porthleven ('Porteven') and Loe Bar.

Winston Graham set his popular Poldark historical novels in Cornwall between 1780 and 1815. The first four (*Ross Poldark, Demelza, Jeremy Poldark* and *Warleggan*) were written in 1945-53, but the books were continued after a successful television series. The eleventh and last, *The Twisted Sword*, was launched in 1990 appropriately at the Poldark Mine and Museum tourist attraction at Wendron. Graham took locations from the area around Perranporth where he lived for several years, while relying strongly on historical fact for the background.

Some names are real figures; others are the author's inventions, such as Poldark himself. Demelza was taken from a hamlet seen signposted near Roche, and Warleggan came from the hamlet on Bodmin Moor. *Poldark's Cornwall* (1983) describes the writing of the books, although it makes much of the television filming.

Ruth Manning-Sanders lived in West Penwith for many years, first at Sennen and then Penzance where she died in 1988 aged 100. A poet and novelist for much of her life, she was known for her short stories on folklore, giants and monsters, and drew on Cornish folklore and legends for some.

This district has remained a popular location for mining and other stories. For example, Hammond Innes's adventure novel *The Killer Mine* (1947) takes place around Botallack after the Second World War, with the key ingredients of smuggling, mining and love. He chose local place names with care, such as Cripples Ease, Ding Dong Mine, Botallack and Kenidjack. *The Black Tide* (1982) was inspired by the Torrey Canyon disaster in 1967, but this story uncovers more than just the wreck of the *Petros Jupiter*.

Writing in a much different style, the Cornish poet D. M. Thomas won international success as a novelist with *The White Hotel* in 1981. His *Birthstone* (1980) is set firmly in West Penwith. This unusual and thought-provoking book is narrated through the eyes of the schizoid Joanne as the action unfolds in and around Pendeen.

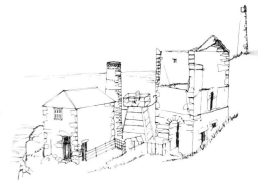

Levant Mine, in a similar cliff-top setting to Wheal Garth of *The Killer Mine* by Hammond Innes.

The family saga *Penmarric* (1971) by Susan Howatch has five narrators over the period 1890-1945, with the fictitious 'Penmarric' placed on the clifftops near St Just. Other houses can be identified, such as 'Menherion Castle' (Tregenna Castle Hotel at St Ives) or 'Gurnard's Grange' (Carnelloe, just west of Zennor).

Popular novelists today include Mary Williams of St Ives, a writer of ghost stories and historical romances. Cornwall and West Penwith are ever present in her novels, such as *The Granite King* (1982) and *Tangled Roots* (1990). *The Mistress of Blackstone* is set against a mining background, while *Folly's End* concerns smuggling in north Cornwall.

E. V. Thompson won an important Best Historical Novel award in 1977 with *Chase the Wind*, a story of mining on the edge of Bodmin Moor in the 1840s. Unusually, he wrote *Ben Retallack* not as a sequel but as a prelude to this family saga which later crossed to South Africa. Thompson, who found inspiration by returning to his Cornish roots, has not kept to mining. For example, *The Restless Sea* (1983) concerns the Jago fishing family of Pentuan and 'Portgiskey' in the early nineteenth century. The sequel is *Polrudden* (1985). Several of Thompson's other novels are set far overseas.

W. J. Burley of Newquay has made a success with his Wycliffe Cornish detective stories since 1966, with county locations used throughout. For example, the Mevagissey area features in a recent addition to the series, *Wycliffe and the Tangled Webb* (1990).

Before his death in 1984, Denys Val Baker spent his Cornish years at many locations in the county, particularly West Penwith. Cornwall permeates his numerous short stories, published in collections such as *The Secret Place*, *Echoes from the Cornish Cliffs* and *Passenger to Penzance* .

AUTOBIOGRAPHIES

Autobiographies are informative not just about the author, but also the Cornwall in which they lived. For example, Welsh-born Denys Val Baker's first autobiography, *The Sea's in the Kitchen* (1962), describes "ten wandering years" in the West Penwith area, living at as many places including Bernard Walke's Old Vicarage at St Hilary. His seven other autobiographies include *Spring at the Land's End* and *An Old Mill by the Stream*. They tell of his life in Cornwall and the trials of editing his *Cornish Review* in 1949-52 and 1966-74, an outlet for poets, writers and others, and his important contribution to Cornwall's literature.

A. L. Rowse's *A Cornish Childhood* (1942) reveals life in and around his home village of Tregonissey near St Austell, up to 1922 when he left to go to Christ Church, Oxford. He also records his first meeting at Fowey with 'Q' when the latter was helping him gain a university scholarship. *A Cornishman at Oxford* was the natural sequel. From the same china clay district, this time further west around St Stephen, the Calvinist poet Jack Clemo wrote the autobiographies *Confessions of a Rebel* (1949) and *The Invading Gospel* (1958).

Ann Treneer, the daughter of a schoolteacher at Gorran down towards the coast, wrote of her childhood in the late nineteenth and early twentieth centuries there and at Caerhays in *Schoolhouse in the Wind* (1944). A later work was *Cornish Years*. She also wrote a biography of Penzance-born Sir Humphry Davy. Daphne du Maurier lived across St Austell Bay, at Fowey, Menabilly and Kilmarth. It is fortunate that she completed a pictorial autobiography just before her death in 1989. *Enchanted Cornwall* explains how she came to write and set the scenes of her Cornish novels. It is a classic book for the literary explorer, with superb photographs illustrating localities used in her novels. Further along the south coast, Howard Spring described finding a house at Mylor in his second autobiography *In the Meantime* (1942). J. C. Trewin, who later edited the *West Country Magazine*, wrote of his early years spent close to the Lizard Point in *Up from the Lizard* (1948). The successor's title, *Down to the Lion*, refers to the Lion Rock at nearby Kynance.

Away in the far west, Cornishman Derek Tangye became world famous for his highly readable Minack Chronicles, which began with

A Gull on the Roof in 1961. They tell of how he and his wife Jeannie dropped out from the rat-race to run a flower farm at Dorminack on the coast near Lamorna: enchantment, flowers, donkeys and always Jeannie, save for *The Evening Gull* (1990) which was written after her death.

Novels can be semi-autobiographical — some more obviously than others — as for example, Hardy's *A Pair of Blue Eyes*, Lawrence's *Kangaroo* or Walmsley's *Love in the Sun*. Personal experiences of course are hidden in many other novelists' works.

Lizard Point, close to the childhood home of J. C. Trewin, and visited by Collins, Tennyson and others.

POETS

Countless poets have drawn inspiration from Cornwall, but just a few can be mentioned here. Many are also novelists or other writers.

John Harris was a true Cornish poet of the nineteenth century. He was born in 1820 at Bolenowe Hill near Camborne, and his best, lengthy poetry was written while still working at Dolcoath Mine. His published collections include *Lays from the Mine, The Moor and the Mountain* and *A Story of Carn Brea*, all influenced by the powerful landscape and the mining industry which it supported. A selection of his poems was republished in 1977 in *Songs from the Earth*. Penzance's son Humphry Davy, the scientist and inventor of the miners' safety lamp, was less famous as a poet but was praised by Coleridge.

The poetry of R. S. Hawker was inspired by the windswept and dangerous coast of his Morwenstow, where he wrote in his clifftop hut. He promoted the Arthurian legends through his 'Quest of the Sangraal', a work which was praised by Tennyson. More poems were published in *Cornish Ballads and Other Poems* in 1869. 'The Song of the Western Men' is his most famous work. The refrain "And shall Trelawny die? Here's 20,000 Cornish men will know the reason why!" was already a well known Cornish proverb, referring to the imprisonment of Jonathan Trelawny and six other bishops by James II. Adapting it, Hawker published his ballad anonymously in the *Royal Devonport Telegraph & Plymouth Chronicle* in 1826. Davies Gilbert contributed it to the *Gentlemans Magazine*, and Dickens even pub-

Figurehead of the *Caledonia*, Morwenstow Churchyard.
"And there, the relique of the storm,
We fixed fair Scotland's figured form."
(R.S. Hawker, 'The Figure-Head of the Caledonia at her Captain's Grave')

lished it in *Household Words*, assuming it to be ancient. Hawker owned up eventually. 'Trelawny', as it is also known, was used as a march by the Duke of Cornwall's Light Infantry and it is now a Cornish national anthem. Of related interest, Baring-Gould's *Songs of the West: Folk Songs of Devon and Cornwall* was "collected from the mouths of the people" by himself and H. Fleetwood Sheppard.

Hawker's poems include legends of the north coast, such as 'The Silent Tower of Bottreaux' about the loss of a ship bearing bells for Forrabury church. Other shipwreck poems relate to true events, one which involved Hawker personally being the *Caledonia*, whose figurehead is in Morwenstow churchyard. 'The Wreck' is that of the Spanish brig *Santa Anna y Santa Josepha* at Bude after nine days and nights of storm in August 1790.

Algernon Charles Swinburne, a writer of much and sometimes controversial verse, was another poet connected with the north Cornish coast, having stayed a while at Tintagel in 1864. His 'Tristram of Lyonesse' was well received years later in 1882.

On a Cornish visit in June 1848, Alfred Lord Tennyson met Hawker at Morwenstow and briefly recorded in his journal: "Coldest manner of Vicar till I told him my name, then all heartiness. Walk on cliff with him, told of shipwreck." Tennyson will always be remembered for his epic Arthurian poem 'Idylls of the King', although this long work contains but few descriptive passages of Tintagel, Loe Pool or Lyonesse. Encouraged by the success of his first 'Idylls', Tennyson toured Cornwall again for more inspiration in August-September 1860, and further sections were added until 1885. 'The Revenge' immortalised Sir Richard Grenville's heroic battle in his tiny ship against the Spanish fleet. The Grenvilles have a north Cornish connection at Stowe, although the Revenge of the ballad was crewed by "men of Bideford in Devon."

Although he first came in 1870, Thomas Hardy's main Cornish poetry dates from the early twentieth century. Cornwall held a special place in his heart, for here he met his first wife Emma and it was she who encouraged his writing. His most exquisite love poems were written after her death forty years later, inspired by memories of their courtship at St Juliot and Boscastle. The poems recall coastal or riverside scenes they visited, such as 'After a Journey', 'At Castle Boterel', 'Beeny Cliff', 'I Found Her Out There' and 'Under the Waterfall'.

Cornish-born poets of the twentieth century include Charles Causley, Jack Clemo, Geoffrey Grigson and D. M. Thomas. A. L. Rowse has been described as the "doyen of Cornish poets" and Cornwall is in many of his poems. Sir John Betjeman was Cornish by adoption, and his great love for Cornwall is seen in his poetry and other writing. The poems 'North Coast Recollections' and 'Trebetherick' recall earlier years when he stayed at Trebetherick.

Charles Causley was born in 1917 at Launceston, where he was educated and returned to teach after war service in the Royal Navy. He has published his own poems, anthologies and children's stories. His *Collected Poems, 1951-75* is representative, and while some poems and ballads have a nautical flavour, many are about Cornwall, Launceston or Bodmin Moor. *Secret Destinations* (1984) is among his more recent collections.

Jack Clemo's Clay Country. "The waggon stiff and derelict" ('Reclaimed')

Jack Clemo was born in 1916 near St Stephen in the china clay district, and lived at Goonamarris until he moved to Weymouth in 1985. Despite later suffering from blindness and deafness, he directed his talents to writing. His Calvinist faith and the "scarred and erie landscape" around him greatly influenced his earlier poetry, contained in his main collections *The Clay Verge* (1951), *The Map of Clay* (1961) and *The Echoing Tip* (1971). Many Dorset poems are in *A Different Drummer* (1986).

Geoffrey Grigson from Pelynt founded and edited the influential magazine *New Verse* in the 1930s. His own poetry includes poems of Cornwall, found for example in *The Isles of Scilly and Other Poems* (1946) and his *Collected Poems 1924-1962*.

D. M. Thomas was born at Redruth in 1935, and is both a novelist and poet. His anthology *The Granite Kingdom* (1970) contains his own works among those of other poets with Cornish connections. The Cornish landscape comes through forcefully in his poems, such as 'Two at Castle Dor', 'Botallack' and and 'Logan-Stone'. He often uses the theme of logan rocks, echoing the delicate balance of life. Indeed, one of his collections is called *Logan Stone* (1971).

Of the many poets who have visited Cornwall, John Heath-Stubbs lived a while near Zennor, where he described the landscape in his poem 'To the Mermaid at Zennor'. Another local poem is 'The Last Will and Testament of the Cornish Chough', which mourns the passing of romantic Cornwall.

Dylan Thomas lived for a period in 1936-7 at Porthcurno, Mousehole and Newlyn, and married Caitlin Macnamara at Penzance. Cornwall did not help his writing. He confessed in his letters he was not a country man, finding the peninsula a strange country, preferring "the bound slope of a suburban hill...to all these miles of green fields and flowery cliffs and dull sea going on and on, and cows lying down and down."

Yorkshire-born Arthur Caddick came to Cornwall in 1945 and lived for thirty-six years at Nancledra in a small cottage which came with the job of attending emergencies at the local electricity sub-station. Caddick contributed to the *Cornish Review* and his poetry on Cornish matters was noted for its wit. *The Call of the West* (1983) is among his Cornish collections.

Peter Redgrove is another modern poet with much written on Cornwall, contained, for example, in *Poems 1954-1987* (1989).

The Cornish Gorsedd

THE LITERARY LANDSCAPE

This is a gazetteer of the Cornish landscape in literature. The eight districts (each with a location map) give an indication of the many places of interest which have appeared in print, or have other associations with writers. Space permits just a summary for the general reader, but it is hoped this will inspire others to look afresh at Cornwall's very strong influence on all types of literature. The more serious reader will be armed with a book or novel when exploring the county, while diaries or travel books make it possible to follow in an author's footsteps.

Note: some places mentioned are private property, although they can often be viewed from a vantage point.

Cornwall showing the location of districts in the gazeteer

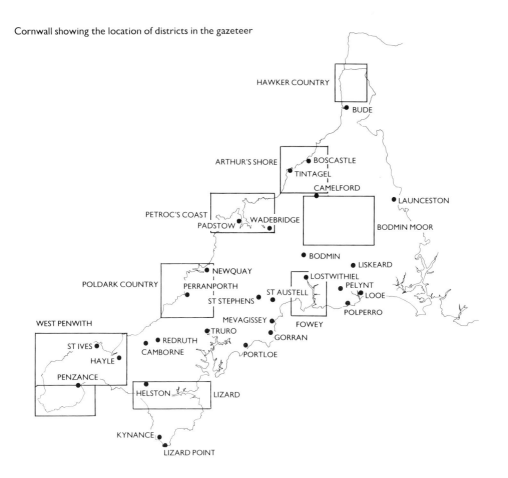

WEST PENWITH

J. T. Blight's *A Week at the Land's End* is still among the best period pieces written on this district. West Penwith is Ruth-Manning Sanders' "all-but-island" where "the sea is almost everywhere in sight, and always within hearing. In times of tempest its long roar fills earth and sky; in times of calm the light winds carry its throb and rumble over fields and moors as if some giant were at work, threshing corn..." (*The West of England*, 1949).

Land's End

LAND'S END

W.H. Hudson observed in *The Land's End* how the actual "end of all the land" does not always match the image anticipated by visitors, for it is surpassed in grandeur by cliffs along the coast. Yet Land's End has always been an essential place of pilgrimage for any visitor to Cornwall, always producing mixed reactions. "It was an awful sight!" John Wesley proclaimed on his first visit in September 1743. This was a busy day,

for he had already risen to preach at four in the morning at Sennen, and was to hold four more services between here and St Ives which he reached by nightfall. He returned at the age of 82 and "clambered down the rocks to the very edge of the water."

Wilkie Collins was shown the shaped rocks known as Dr Johnson's and Dr Syntax's Heads in 1850. He could not see Johnson in the for-

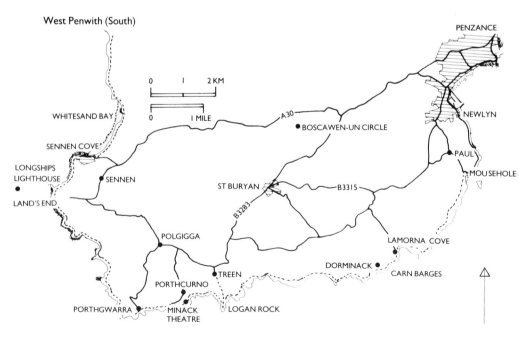

West Penwith (South)

mer, but instead found "in violent exaggeration, the worst physiognomical peculiarites of Nero and Henry the Eighth, combined in one face!" Other visiting diarists and travellers included Walter White, who was rather disappointed, and Mrs Craik, who found the place "stimulating." Tennyson stayed here at a "rackity, rather dirty inn" in 1860. Like Collins twenty years before him, Francis Kilvert noted the "first milestone, inscribed with 'I' as if it were the original mile in England."

Charles Dickens and his party explored this area at the end of October 1842, and he included a passage in *A Christmas Carol* where the Ghost of the Christmas Present took Scrooge to "a bleak and desert moor, where monstrous masses of rude stone were cast about, as though it were the burial place of the giants..." The ghost showed him the keepers wishing themselves a Merry Christmas in a lighthouse "built upon a dismal reef of sunken rocks, some league or so from the shore."

Dickens's lighthouse was the Longships, which stands on the Carn Brâs rock 1¼ miles off Land's End. J. F. Cobb's novel *The Watchers on the Longships* concerns the problems of erecting and manning this precarious lighthouse, interwoven with smuggling and wrecking. Blight confirmed true elements in the tale, like a keeper's hair turning white overnight during a terrifying storm in which the lantern was smashed by the waves. That first lighthouse of 1795 was replaced by the present taller one in 1873. Cobb made Sennen the home of Owen Tresilian, the first keeper whose brave daughter Mary was trapped alone in the lighthouse in a storm but managed to keep the light burning.

Trouble at the Longships Lighthouse "The Bible was placed on the chair, and over it the basin, upon which Mary climbed" (J.F. Cobb, *Watchers on the Longships*)

The final shipwreck was on Sennen beach, where the preacher and lighthouse promoter Arthur Pendrean died while rescuing Philip Tresilian from the surf. Ruth Manning-Sanders, who lived at Sennen, described the "solitary watcher — the red, rhythmically winking eye" of the Longships.

The first Longships Lighthouse, described by Charles Dickens and J. F. Cobb

West Penwith (north)

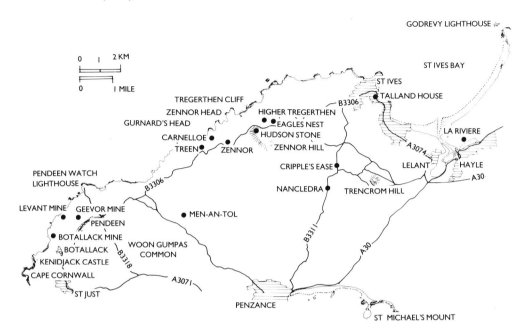

LYONESSE

Beneath the waves offshore lies the legendary lost Lyonesse with its 140 churches, while the scattered Isles of Scilly stand plain on the horizon on a clear day. After his Cornish visit, Collins sailed there in a cutter from the Bristol Channel and gave a brief description. Tennyson took a shorter voyage from Penzance and "never saw anything quite like them." The islands were the 'Isles of Lyonesse' in Hardy's *A Brief Interlude*. St Mary's was 'St Maria's' and Hugh Town was 'Giant's Town', although he gave no real description. Geoffrey Grigson knew the Isles of Scilly well and wrote two books, one descriptive and the other of poetry. Of novels, Walter Besant and 'Q' used the islands for their *Armorel of Lyonesse* and *Major Vigoureux*.

ST JUST AND BOTALLACK

North-east of Land's End, the mining district around St Just has fascinated several writers. The famous Botallack Mine ran from the cliffs out under the sea, and Wilkie Collins described his descent in fearsome terms for his readers. Charles Dickens probably visited it too, but Walter White declined the opportunity! R. M. Ballantyne wove the adventures of Oliver Trembath around the mine in *Deep Down*, giving descriptions of its workings, accidents including holing into a 'House of Water', and miners' tombstones at St Just. Oliver stayed with his uncle in "one of the most respectable of the group of old houses" near St Just parish church.

Hammond Innes' *Killer Mine* is set along these

"The last look at the sun" before descending Botallack Mine (R.M. Ballantyne, *Deep Down*)

The Hudson Rock on the seaward slope of Zennor Hill

cliffs in the 1940s. There are gripping underground scenes, especially when the bitter old Manack deliberately loses the Cornish hero Jim Pryce in the old workings of Wheal Garth. As in Ballantyne's book, disaster strikes when a 'House of Water' is holed, but this time the act is more sinister.

St Just is also the country of Susan Howatch's *Penmarric*, with the 'Penmarric' property "a castle built on cliffs facing the sea" to the southwest of the village. The rich 'Sennen Garth' tin mine is towards Cape Cornwall. D. M. Thomas's very different *Birthstone* is set mainly around Pendeen, and includes the Pendeen Watch lighthouse.

ZENNOR

Zennor has many literary associations. W. H. Hudson wintered here in 1906-7, staying in a small cottage in the centre of what is still "that lonely little village nestling among its furze thickets and stone hedges, with rough granite hills, clothed in brown dead bracken, before it and the black granite cliffs and sea behind." From this stay came *The Land's End*, which describes the natural history as well as contemporary life at St. Ives, Penzance and surrounding villages of West Penwith. Hudson was drawn back to the

area towards the end of his life. In 1921 he visited Will Arnold-Forster in his home at Eagle's Nest, perched beside the coast road at Tregerthen Hill. It was Arnold-Forster who had the inscription 'WH HUDSON OFTEN CAME HERE' carved on a rock face of the first main tor on the north slope of Zennor Hill. Hudson is said to have sat here in solitude and thought, a place with panoramic views along the coast and far out to sea. The rock is not easy to reach from the road below, but the interested explorer will find this lonely memorial worth finding.

Below Eagle's Nest is Higher Tregerthen, where D. H. Lawrence and his German-born wife Frieda rented three cottages during the Great War. His later book *Kangaroo* describes his Cornish experiences and this stay at 'Trevetham Cottage' through the eyes of Richard Somers. Harrassment from the military authorities and suspicions of being spies signalling to German submarines were not helped by the wreck of a Spanish collier below the cliffs (the 2,060 ton *Manu* which ran aground in fog on 20th May 1916). He also described the fulfilment of working on a farm here. When given three days to leave Cornwall, Somers determined to return. "His very soul seemed to have sunk into that Cornwall, that wild place under the moors."

In 1919, Virginia and Leonard Woolf rented Lawrence's cottages from Captain Short of St Ives, but it is unclear if they kept the place for long or ever stayed here. Virginia's diary records the exciting prospect of returning to Cornwall, which she had loved since her childhood. On the last evening of a week lodging with a Mrs Hoskings at Zennor in March 1921, she wrote "This is the loveliest place in the world. It is so lonely. Occasionally a very small field is being ploughed, the men steering the plough round the grey granite rocks." Like Hudson, she also knew Arnold-Forster through his marriage to her friend Ka Cox in 1918. She visited them at Eagle's Nest, where she noted "lots of nice elderly men to be seen there, come for climbing," perhaps remembering her own father's love of the sport.

Zennor's rocky moorland hills were Ranger Gull's "Hinterland" and Folliott -Stokes's"Cornish Connemara". The poet John Heath-Stubbs stayed in a coastguard cottage at Gurnard's Head. He too felt the mystery of the landscape, writing

"This is a hideous and wicked country
Sloping to hateful sunsets and the end of time,"

('To the Mermaid at Zennor')

ST IVES BAY

Like its artists, St Ives has been home to a number of writers too. Virginia Woolf's first relationship with Cornwall was as a child, holidaying at her father Sir Leslie Stephen's Talland House, off Talland Road in St Ives. Although she set *To the Lighthouse* in the Hebrides, the family, house and view across the bay (before it was obscured by buildings) are clear descriptions of St Ives and its bay. Early this century, Mrs Havelock Ellis (Edith Ellis) lived in a converted mine count house at Carbis Bay, where she wrote *My Cornish Neighbours*. C. Ranger Gull (Guy Thorne) also lived there. His book *Portalone* (1904) tells of artists in the fishing community of an undisguised St. Ives. His friend A.G. Folliot-Stokes based his characters on the same people at "St Ars" in his story *The Moorland Princess: A Romance of Lyonesse* (1904). Charles Marriott lived in Porthminster Terrace, St Ives (his 'Porthia'), where he was visited by W. H. Hudson (who wrote of the ill-treatment of birds here), Hugh Walpole and Compton Mackenzie. In more recent years, St Ives has been the home of Mary Williams and Roy Phillips, whose *The Saffron Eaters* (1987) is set around the area and won the TSB Peninsula Prize for best unpublished novel.

Across St Ives Bay, the Godrevy lighthouse on its rocky island is the one of Virginia' Woolf's book. Nearby, Marriott's *The House on the Sands* (1903) was 'Chy-an-dreath', a tin streamer's house beside the Red River at Gwithian. Compton Mackenzie wrote his first novel *Carnival* when he was living in 1908-10 at La Riviere, the rectory at Phillack (Hayle) visited and

Talland House, St Ives, once the home of Sir Leslie Stephen and his daughter Virginia Woolf.

Mousehole "...really the loveliest village in England." (Dylan Thomas)

described by Kilvert in 1870. Back in the 1780s, Hayle received acclaim when John Wesley twice praised the walls of the new preaching-house as being made of 'brass' (slag blocks from the copper smelting works at Copperhouse).

LOGAN ROCK

Along the south coast, the Logan Rock at Treryn Dinas was a place on most Victorians' itineraries when on their way to Land's End. It was famous before Goldsmith overturned and replaced the rock in 1824, but his actions no doubt increased the tourist interest. Indeed, such was its popularity with the masses by 1870 that Kilvert could write "a rude vulgar crew of tourists (real British) passed us going down to the cliffs, grinning like dogs..." Forster sat on the top of the stone while the others rocked it when Dickens and his party came here in October 1842. Palgrave followed Tennyson here in 1860, and in his dedication to him in *The Golden Treasury*, he wrote: "Your encouragement, given while traversing the wild scenery of Treryn Dinas, led me to begin the work; and it has been completed under your advice and assistance."

Wilkie Collins described the 'Loggan Rock' in his *Rambles*, and used the district in his novel *Basil*. Having fled his enemy Robert Mannion, Basil stayed in a fishing hamlet (Porthgwarra?), but

was followed two months later. Although unnamed, it was the rocky headland of Treryn Dinas where Mannion confronted Basil and fell to his death. The shocked Basil was cared for at the inn at Treen before his brother and sister fetched him home.

LAMORNA COVE

The use of real place-names such as Carn Mellyn and Carn Bargis suggests that Lamorna was the 'Polurrian Cove' of Joseph Pearce's *Ezekial's Sin*, a tale of Ezekial Trevaskis who was a crabber along this coast. A place for artists, Lamorna was also home for a while to the novelist Crosbie Garstin before he moved inland to St Buryan (the 'St Gwithian' of his Penhale trilogy). Charles Marriott stayed in 1901-2 at Flagstaff Cottage, which was then taken by his friend the artist Lamorna Birch. Dylan Thomas and Caitlin Macnamara also stayed here in a cottage before moving to Mousehole in 1937. Just along the cliffs to the west is Dorminack, made famous by Derek Tangye's *Minack Chronicles*.

MOUNT'S BAY

Mousehole, Newlyn and Penzance are the three ports which cling to the west corner of Mount's Bay. Up on the hill above Mousehole is the parish church of Paul, with its monument to Dolly Pentreath, the reputed last Cornish-speaker. In 1937, Dylan Thomas and Caitlin Macnamara stayed at The Lobster Pot in Mousehole, which he called "really the loveliest village in England." From here they married quietly at Penzance registry office in July 1937, and rented a studio at Newlyn "above a fish-market and where gulls fly in for breakfast." Cornwall does not seem to have influenced his writing. Nevertheless, Newlyn inspired other writers at the time of its famous school of artists. For example, it is in Charles Lee's *The Widow Woman*, Joseph Pearce's *Inconsequent Lives* and Eden Phillpott's *Lying Prophets*.

Penzance was 'Pen-zephyr' in Thomas Hardy's short story *A Mere Interlude*. Here, Baptista Trewthen's first husband was drowned after their secret marriage in 'Trufal', and a few nights later she and her second husband shared a room next to the body. Hardy kept the names of Mousehole and St Clements Isle. Crosbie Garstin was born at Alexandra Road in 1887. Humphry Davy, whose statue looks down Market Jew Street, was a poet as well as a scientist and inventor of the miners' safety lamp. The Brontë sisters' mother and aunt came from Penzance, where their father Thomas Branwell had a house at 25 Chapel Street.

THE LIZARD

North border of the Lizard, between Loe Bar and the Helford

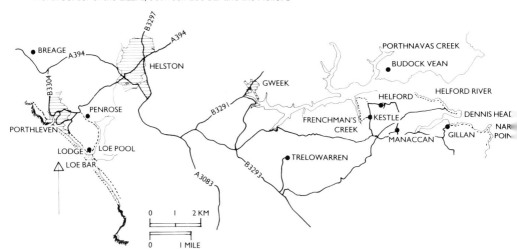

The Lizard peninsula is a prominent feature on the map of Cornwall, which Daphne du Maurier called "the southern grip of Cornwall's claw, its pincher probing the Channel at Lizard Point..." To Kilvert, its windswept plateau top was a "wild strange treeless district." As with Land's End and Blight's delightful book, this district has the Rev C. A. Johns's *A Week at the Lizard*.
Many ·tourists and travellers have visited the Lizard too. For example, Tennyson came in July

1848. The "two southern eyes of England" in his journal refer to the Lizard's twin lighthouse towers (only one has been lit since 1903). He swam at Polpeor ('Polpur') Cove, went to Kynance and rowed into the narrow cleft beyond called Pigeon Ogo. He returned in September 1860, where he and Palgrave left Hunt and Prinsep "hard at work sketching on a promontory."

In 1850, Wilkie Collins described following

Trelowarren House, home of C. C. Vyvyan

paths along the tops of thick stone field walls as he and Henry Brandling went down to view the cliff scenery on either side of the Lizard, including Pistol Meadow and the Lion's Den. Kynance Cove was "a perfect palace of rocks," where a guide took them on an adventurous visit to Asparagus Island to see the Devil's Bellows (blowhole). Few visitors had kind words for the Lizard's main settlement. Collins suggested that whoever named the group of cottages "Lizard *Town* must have possessed magnificent ideas indeed on the subject of nomenclature." They found an inn, but on entering a room found it full of babies about to be vaccinated against smallpox by a local doctor, who "sent us out of the house without a moment's delay!" Soon after, Walter White found Lizard Town "a poor scattered village, with one tavern recently built for the entertainment of visitors."

Kenneth Grahame's first Cornish visit was to the Lizard in August 1884. He came with his sister (who later bought a house here), and was much taken by the rugged coast, wild seas and the Cornish people.

J. C. Trewin, the son of a sea captain, was brought up in a house called Kynance Bay, standing in an exposed position close to the Lizard Point. This he described in his autobiographical *Up from the Lizard*.

Tucked away in the north part of the peninsula,

Trelowarren House was C. C. Vyvyan's home, which she described in her *Letters from a Cornish Garden* and *The Old Place*. Lady Vyvyan also wrote *Our Cornwall*. Trelowarren can be visited by the public.

The Lizard peninsula is joined to the rest of Cornwall by a narrow neck between the Helford River and the once tidal Loe Pool. The remoter reaches of the Helford estuary are places of enchantment and mystery. The hero of Charles Kingsley's *Hereward the Wake* first came with merchants bringing wine to trade for tin, sailing "over a rolling bar, between jagged points of black rock, and up a tidal river which wandered and branched away inland like a landlocked lake, between green walls of oak and ash, till they saw at the head of the tide Alef's town [Gweek]." The second time, Hereward rescued a princess at Gweek and escaped by a three-day circuitous route to three waiting ships in "a little cove beyond Marazion."

Overlooking Porthnavas Creek on the north side of the Helford, the Budock Vean Hotel would seem to be the "Tresco Vean" of Howard Spring's *There is no Armour*. On the south side, Daphne du Maurier's famous *Frenchman's Creek* (a title borrowed with permission from 'Q') is "still and soundless, shrouded by the trees, hidden from the eyes of men... this stealthy branch of the parent river."

Frenchman's Creek "...still and soundless, shrouded by the trees..." (Daphne du Maurier, *Frenchman's Creek*)

Here the French pirate Jean-Benoit Aubery hid his vessel *La Mouette*, to be discovered by the heroine Dona St Columb, lady of Navron House. Dennis Head or Nare Point would be the 'sloping headland' from which Dona first saw the ship steal in towards the land at sunset. The Frenchman escaped from Loe Bar, the last scene in the book.

Loe Bar and Pool are said to be the spot envisaged by Tennyson in his 'Morte d'Arthur'. When Arthur was mortally wounded by Mordred in Lyonesse, Sir Bedivere bore him to a ruined chapel

"That stood on a dark strait of barren land.
On one side lay the Ocean, and on one
Lay a great water..."

Arthur bade the reluctant Bedivere to throw Excalibur into the lake. At the third attempt, an arm rose to catch the sword by the hilt, brandished it three times "and drew him under in the mere." Then Bedivere carried his king to the lake where a barge waited with three queens to carry Arthur away.

As with many of Cornwall's atmospheric places, the best time to come here is on a stormy winter's day. Even in summer, Wilkie Collins found "the surf forbade all hope of swimming; but...where the spray flew highest before the wind, I could take a natural shower-bath from the sea, in one direction; and the next moment, turning round in the other, could wash the sand off my feet luxuriously in the soft, fresh waters of Loo Pool."

The earlier part of Howard Spring's *The Houses in Between* was set around the bar, pool, the estate and house at Penrose ('Tresant') and Porthleven ('Porteven'). The narrator Sarah Undridge, who lived to 99, said "the bar and the road to it are always for me the loveliest things at Tresant...the woods and the lake, the bar and the sea..." This is now National Trust property and, although the house is not open, Sarah's favourite walk to the bar can be followed. The lodge house (Bar Lodge) overlooking the sea and bar was Eddy Rodda's cottage in the book, and the bar itself the scene of a shipwreck and lifeboat disaster when Lord Burnage (Sarah's step-father) was paralysed while bravely rescuing Rodda.

Trevaunance Cove, in the heart of Poldark Country.

POLDARK COUNTRY

This is all mining country, spanning the narrowest part of Cornwall between Perranporth on the north coast and Falmouth in the south. It is bounded on the west by the great mining district around Camborne and Redruth, while far off to the east are the 'Cornish Alps' of the St Austell china clay district.

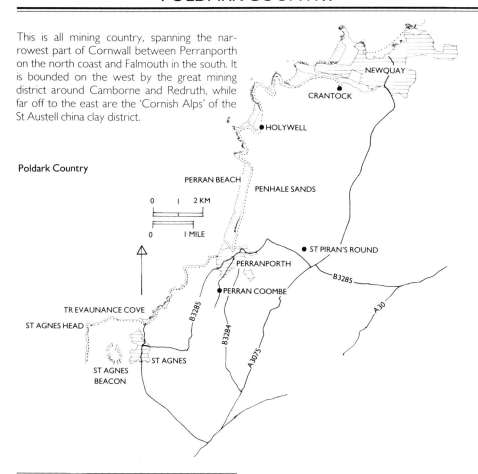

Poldark Country

NORTH COAST

The area around Perranporth and St Agnes is closely identified with Winston Graham's *Poldark* novels. Towns like Truro and Falmouth are given their real names and described with historical accuracy, but along this north coast 'Nampara', 'Sawle', 'St Annes' (St Agnes) and 'Hendrawna Beach' (Perran Beach) are all composites. One cannot always place a site precisely, but exploring the whole area between St Agnes Head and Crantock, seeking out the old parts and ruined mines, brings one closest to the atmosphere of the novels. A useful impression of this imagined landscape was given by a map of 'Poldark Country 1783-93' which was published in the Collins Quartet of the first four novels. Graham wrote *Demelza* in a small wooden bungalow which he rented across the beach from Perranporth. He was then living nearby at Perran Coombe.

Back in 1860, Palgrave walked with Tennyson from Truro to Perranporth, "a little village on the coast, which here was a stretch of level golden sands, barred at each end by fine rocks." A little inland is St Piran's Round, "hard by the edge of the sand-hills, and close beside the high road on the last rise before it dips to the coast."

('Q') The road is the B3285. This circular earth-work was visited in 1850 by Wilkie Collins, who described the ancient Cornish drama once performed here.

Further along the coast, Crantock and Newquay were the locations for G. Norway's *A True Cornish Maid* (1894), the ingredients of which include the pilchard fishery, piskies, smuggling and the tea caverns where Honor Chegwidden's brother Philip hid from the press gang. W. J. Burley, the author of the Wycliffe Cornish detective novels taught at Newquay before retiring to write at nearby Holywell.

CARN BREA

Carn Brea "How the great mountain like a rocky king stands silent in the tempest!" (John Harris, 'A Story of Carn Brea')

The long granite hill of Carn Brea dominates the few miles between Camborne and Redruth. John Wesley went for a rare stroll here between preaching in September 1770, and recorded the "Druid altars of enormous size, being only huge rocks, strangely suspended one upon the other." Commenting on their great antiquity, he concluded "And what are they the better for this? Of what consequence is it, either to the dead or the living, whether they have withstood the wastes of time for three thousands or three hundred years?" Below the neighbouring but smaller Carn Marth was his favourite preaching place at Gwennap Pit, "the most magnificent spectacle to be seen this side of heaven." Altered since his time, this hollow among the mine workings has been terraced as a memorial to a great man.

Carn Brea was the hill of the poet John Harris, who hailed this "rude ridge of boulders, carn of polish'd crag!" He was born nearby at Bolenowe Hill and several of his poems concern the area, its people and its mines, 'A Story of Carn Brea' being the best. This is the heart of the mining district, and in 1855 Walter White described the prospect from Carn Brea as "a hungry landscape, everywhere deformed by small mountains of many-coloured refuse; traversed in all directions by narrow paths and winding roads, by streams of foul water...the stamping-mills appear to try which can thunder the loudest, proclaiming afar the progress made in disembowelling the bountiful earth."

The view from Carn Brea down towards the coast and the hills of West Penwith is tremendous. Charles Marriott discovered his 'real Cornwall' from here in 1889, and the summit is still a place of giants, solitude and inspiration.

Gwennap Pit, John Wesley preached here in August 1773, "perhaps the first time that a man of seventy had been heard by thirty thousand persons at once."

FOWEY

Many days can be spent exploring the literary heritage in and around this Cornish seaport whose most celebrated authors are Sir Arthur Quiller-Couch ('Q') and Daphne du Maurier. 'Q' first saw Fowey as a schoolboy in 1879 and decided then to make it his home, which he did in 1892, having married Louisa Hicks here in 1889. By then, he had been to Oxford University and begun writing in London to pay off his father's debts. He lived at Fowey until his death in 1944, although his residence was interrupted during term-time after 1912 when he was appointed Professor of English Literature at Cambridge. He contributed fully to life at Fowey, becoming a magistrate, Chairman of the Harbour Commissioners and Commodore of the Fowey Yacht Club.

He called Fowey his 'Troy', making fun of the inhabitants in his second novel, *The Astonishing History of Troy Town*. His house The Haven is near the Polruan ferry pier at Whitehouse Point, overlooking his beloved harbour which, as in his day, is still busy with shipping and sailing boats. *From a Cornish Window* describes the scene, looking out "upon a small harbour frequented by ships of all nations — British, Danish, Swedish, Norwegian, Russian, French, German, Italian, with now and then an American or Greek — and upon a shore which I love because it is my native country. Of all views I reckon that of a harbour the most fascinating and the most easeful, for it combines perpetual change with perpetual repose." He was insistent

that Fowey was not the "little fishing town" as he had so often read in guide books.

'Q' became friends with Kenneth Grahame when the latter was convalescing from pnuemonia at the Fowey Hotel in 1899. It was from The Haven that Grahame was married in Fowey church that summer. 'Q' and Grahame rowed together on the river, so it is of no surprise that in *The Wind in the Willows* the Sea Rat is speaking of Fowey when he describes "the little grey sea town I know so well, that clings along one steep side of the harbour. There through dark doorways you look down flights of stone steps, overhung by great pink tufts of valerian and ending in a patch of sparkling blue water. The little boats that lie tethered to the rings and stanchions of the old sea-wall

Fowey Peninsula

The Haven at Fowey. "My window, then, looks out from a small library upon a small harbour frequented by ships of all nations...As for the house, it is a plain one; indeed, very like the house a child draws on a slate..." ('Q', *From a Cornish Window*)

are gaily painted...and by the windows the great vessels glide, night and day, up to their moorings or forth to the open sea." As with 'Q', he could be describing Fowey today.

The best circular 'literary walk' in Cornwall encompasses the whole harbour, crossing first by ferry from Fowey to Bodinnick, thence by footpath around Pont Pill to Polruan, and returning by a second ferry to the town. Upstream from the little car ferry to Bodinnick are the busy jetties where ships of all nations still load china clay, while others may wait in the river here or opposite the Town Quay. At the first great river bend is Mixtow Pill, where Mr Fogo rented Kit's House in *The Astonishing History of Troy Town*. Out of sight and further up-river near Golant, Denys Val Baker once lived at an old sawmill, the subject of *An Old Mill by a Stream*.

Q's view of Polruan ('Ruan') from beside The Haven. .

Next to the ferry slip at Bodinnick, Ferryside was the home of Daphne du Maurier, bought when her family came to Cornwall in 1926. The figurehead of the local schooner *Jane Slade* is fixed on the seaward corner. It was the boat-building Slade family of Polruan who inspired du Maurier's first Cornish novel *The Loving Spirit*, a romantic story following several generations of the Coombe family of 'Plyn' (Polruan). Here at Ferryside she also wrote her famous novels *Jamaica Inn*, *Rebecca* and *Frenchman's Creek*.

A path leads from above the Old Ferry Inn to Hall Walk (the 'King's Walk' of 'Q'), which was given to the National Trust in memory of 'Q' and the men of Fowey and Lanteglos who fell in the Second World War. A granite memorial above Penleath Point was dedicated to 'Q' in 1948. From here there are striking views seawards over the harbour and town, exactly the scene back in 1602 when Richard Carew wrote "Foy subjecteth his whole length and breadth to your overlooking: and directly under you ride the home and forraine shipping..." Below Hall Walk is the overgrown orchard and garden which 'Q' called The Farm, to which he rowed over frequently from Fowey. He was nearly killed here in 1941 when German bombs missed shipping in the harbour.

The path continues above Pont Pill, a branch of the harbour. On the opposite shore is the old red-roofed isolation hospital where Lewis Hind saw a Russian Finn recovering from typhoid early this century (*Days in Cornwall*). An old army hut further upstream was home to Leo Walmsley in the 1930s and 1950s. His book *Love in the Sun* described discovering and living here, although Fowey was called 'St Jude'. The SS *Heather Wyke* was laid up in the creek and he wrote of other ships laying up in the depression of the 1930s. This was repeated in the late 1950s and early 1960s when tankers and freighters were laid-up at the buoys below Hall Walk. The muddy shore of Pont Pill has been a graveyard for abandoned vessels. Walmsley's broken hulk of the *Amelia Hoskins* would be the same as du Maurier's *Jane Slade* or *Janet Coombe*.

From Pont at the head of the creek, a path climbs to Lanteglos church to which Daphne du Maurier came to be married by boat from Ferryside. It is the 'Lanoc' church in *The Loving Spirit* and here are the graves of the Slades, or

Coombes of the novel. Finally, there is Polruan, the 'Ruan' or 'quaint Penpoodle' of 'Q', Walmsley's 'Porthkerris' (where he placed J. Hoskins & Sons' boatyard), or du Maurier's 'Plyn' (her Coombes' boatyard). The Polruan ferry returns to Fowey, giving a good view from the harbour of The Haven which stands just above the landing pier.

Ferryside at Bodinnick was Daphne du Maurier's home in 1926-1943.

The Fowey estuary reaches far inland and the peninsula between this and St Austell Bay has special associations with Daphne du Maurier. West of Fowey is Menabilly, the house and estate to which she moved in 1943. She had long loved the house, and made the site the 'Manderley' of *Rebecca*. Her first novel written here was *The King's General*, a tale of a long affair between Sir Richard Grenville and the crippled Honor Harris who resided here through the troubled times of the Civil War. The book is based on the memoirs of Honor Harris, whose memorial tablet is in Tywardreath church. Down below Menabilly is the cove at Polridmouth, or Pridmouth, from which Grenville escaped by boat, and where Rebecca had her boat house and died.

Daphne du Maurier was never far from the sea. She spent the last years of her life from 1967 to 1989 at nearby Kilmarth, overlooking St Austell Bay. It was here in *The House on the Strand* that a drug sent Dick Young back in time to the domaine of the Champernownes, with many scenes set here and around Tywardreath and Treesmill.

Beside the main road descending into Fowey, is the inscribed Longstone or Tristan Stone, and further along the ridgeway is Castle Dore, a hillfort closely connected with the Tristan le-

Shipping in Fowey Harbour "...a small harbour frequented by ships of all nations..." ('Q')

gends. It features in *Castle Dor* (a novel by 'Q', which du Maurier finished), which relives the legend in the mid-nineteenth century. Many places exist, such as Castle Dore, the scene of the horse races where Amyot saves Linnet, Penquite (now a Youth Hostel), Woodget Pyll and Lantyan opposite St Winnow church. All the time Dr Carfax is unravelling the old legend until the story reaches a climax further inland at the great hillfort of Castle-an-Dinas overlooking the Goss Moor.

'Q' Memorial, Hall Walk, Fowey "By his genius as an author and as an editor he enriched the literature of England and brought honour to his county and to Fowey his home for over fifty years...Courteous in manner, charitable in judgment, chivalrous in action..."

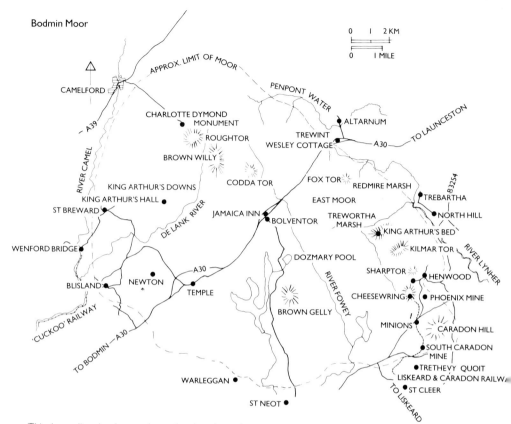

Bodmin Moor

0 1 2 KM
0 1 MILE

APPROX. LIMIT OF MOOR

PENPONT WATER

CAMELFORD

A39

RIVER CAMEL

CHARLOTTE DYMOND MONUMENT

ROUGHTOR

BROWN WILLY

TO LAUNCESTON

ALTARNUM

TREWINT WESLEY COTTAGE

A30

B3254

KING ARTHUR'S DOWNS

KING ARTHUR'S HALL

ST BREWARD

DE LANK RIVER

CODDA TOR

FOX TOR

REDMIRE MARSH

EAST MOOR

TREBARTHA

NORTH HILL

JAMAICA INN

BOLVENTOR

TREWORTHA MARSH

KING ARTHUR'S BED

KILMAR TOR

RIVER LYNHER

WENFORD BRIDGE

DOZMARY POOL

SHARPTOR

HENWOOD

BLISLAND

NEWTON

A30

TEMPLE

RIVER FOWEY

CHEESEWRING

PHOENIX MINE

'CUCKOO' RAILWAY

BROWN GELLY

MINIONS

CARADON HILL

TO BODMIN — A30

SOUTH CARADON MINE

TRETHEVY QUOIT

LISKEARD & CARADON RAILWAY

WARLEGGAN

ST CLEER

TO LISKEARD

ST NEOT

This brooding landscape has stimulated much literary comment, novels and poetry. "These moors have a fascination unlike any other, they are a survival from another age," wrote Daphne du Maurier, a point echoed by James Turner who wrote of the "fierce healing power" of Bodmin Moor: "Here is the last silence of pools and the haunts of neolithic civilization, when man had not lost touch with nature, and spoke the language of cattle and grasses."

CROSSING THE MOOR

For those early travellers entering Cornwall at Launceston there was but a rough track across the great wilderness to Bodmin. John Wesley came this way. On 29th August 1743, he re-corded: "About sunset we were in the middle of the first, great, pathless moor beyond Launceston. About eight we were got quite out of our way. But we had not gone far before we heard Bodmin bell. Directed by this, we turned to the left, and came to the town before nine." The weather was very different the following April, after staying the night at Trewint. "In the morning Diggory Isbell undertook to pilot us over the great Moor, all the paths being covered with snow, which in many places was driven together, too deep for horse or man to pass. The hail followed us for the first seven miles; we had then a fair, though exceeding sharp day." He travelled on, to preach at Gwennap Pit in the evening. The bogs of the trackless moor can be dangerous, even fatal as Baring-Gould nearly found in 1891.

JAMAICA INN

Daphne du Maurier and her friend Foy Quiller-Couch stayed at Jamaica Inn at Bolventor in November 1930, a visit leading to the book *Jamaica Inn*. The place is now a popular tourist venue, and a reconstructed room contains du Maurier's writing desk and other memorabilia. Over the porch is the window of Mary Yelland's bedroom, from which she saw contraband being unloaded from waggons in the yard

Dozmary Pool and Brown Gelly "...a melancholy moorland lake, with the bleak hill above it..." (Mrs Craik, *An Unsentimental Journey Through Cornwall*)

Jamaica Inn at Bolventor "...nothing but the one grim landmark that was Jamaica Inn." (Daphne du Maurier, *Jamaica Inn*)

below. Mary's first adventure on the moor was when she followed her uncle Joss Merlyn to Brown Willy, losing her way when avoiding a marsh, but meeting and falling in love with Joss's brother Jem, a horse thief.

In 1930, Jamaica Inn was still a temperance inn. Baring-Gould earlier described it as "a pleasant little inn...but the visitor must take with him his own supply of liquor." However, Lewis Hind was not impressed when cycling across the moor in 1907. "The hostelry looked as if man had never crossed the grass-grown forecourt," and he found a forbidding woman who plainly desired no guest that night. "I inspected the comfortless sitting room and decided to continue my journey," he concluded.

DOZMARY POOL

Just to the south is Dozmary Pool, which Norden described as "a stange or Poole on the topp of a greate hill, being about a mile in circuit..." and nowhere more than 1½ fathoms deep. Local tradition, rather than literature, has it that Sir Bedivere flung Excalibur into this pool.

Hawker described the pool "with its rippling laugh of waters." In *The Splendid Spur* ('Q'), Jack Marvel twice passed this "broad, dismal sheet of water" as he was chased on horseback, and each time he was nearly caught in a bog here. He escaped to "a clump of roofless cabins" at the shrunken village of Temple where Joan o'the Tor saved him twice, the second time by giving her life.

TWELVE MENS MOOR

Charles Causley's poem 'On Launceston Castle' describes the moor's rocky eastern skyline as "a cardiograph of granite." One of the ridges is Treworrtha Tor, where a curious rock basin is called King Arthur's Bed, but the greatest ridge is Kilmar Tor, below which Jem had his home in *Jamaica Inn*. Daphne du Maurier and Foy Quiller-Couch were caught out in a storm and lost hereabouts when riding from Jamaica Inn to Trebartha Hall in 1930. Mary Yelland took a similar route to find Jem in the book. In *A Book of Cornwall*, Baring-Gould described how he was nearly lost in a bog at Redmire in this same area. "All at once I sank above my waist, and was being sucked further down. I cried to my companion, but in the darkness he could not see me, and had he seen me he could have done nothing for me. The water was up to my armpits. Happily I had a stout bamboo, some six feet long, and I placed this athwart the surface and held it with my arms as far expanded as possible. By jerks I gradually succeeded in lifting myself and throwing my body forward, till finally I was able to cast myself full length on the surface. The suction had been so great as to tear the leather gaiters I wore off my legs..."

CHEESEWRING

The Cheesewring "...a heap of pretty large rocks, under which is a great stone, formed so like a cheese, that it seems to be pressed by the others..." (William Camden)

The popular and celebrated rock formation of the Cheesewring stands on an airy summit above a quarry ("the wicked moor where seven smashed stones lie" of Causley's poem 'Christ at the Cheesewring'). Wilkie Collins called it "the wildest and most wondrous of all the wild and wondrous structures in the rock architecture of the scene. If a man dreamt of a great pile of stones in a nightmare, he would dream of such a pile as the Cheese-Wring." He was ambushed by some tipsy Liskeard tradesmen waving porter bottles as olive branches of peace and goodwill. One "violently uncorked a bottle and directed half of its contents in a magnificent jet of light brown froth all over everybody, before he found the way into the tumbler." Collins had earlier been unimpressed with Liskeard's hostelries too. Below the Cheesewring is Daniel Gumb's Cave, whose life was described by Hawker in a rather fanciful account in *Footprints*.

Trethevy Quoit, near St Cleer. "...when we left Trethevey Stone, we still continued to ascend, proceeding along the tram-way leading to the Caraton Mine." (Wilkie Collins, *Rambles Beyond Railways*)

Ruined engine houses are now the gaunt reminders that this was a busy mining district in the nineteenth century. In his *Rambles*, Collins gave a good description of South Caradon Mine at work as he followed the Liskeard & Caradon Railway after visiting Trethevy Quoit. More recently, E. V. Thompson wrote *Chase the Wind* while living in a cottage at Sharptor near Henwood, and used the history of the local Phoenix mines as the background to this story of Josh Retallack and Miriam Trago. After travelling to Africa the family saga returns in the 1860s to this district and the Sharptor Mine in *Lottie Trago* (1990).

ROUGHTOR AND BLISLAND

Brown Willy from Catshole Tor "Mary plunged on in trail of her uncle...and she could just make out his figure amongst the black heather and the great boulders at the foot of Brown Willy." (Daphne du Maurier, *Jamaica Inn*)

Cornwall's two highest summits are on the north moor, in the parish of St Breward. These are Norden's "Brown-wellye" and "Row-torr — a verie high, spatious, and craggy rocke sett upon a loftye hill." The former inspired the Rev A. N. Malan's novel *Lost on Brown Willy or the Print of the Cloven Hoof* (1890), surely the most classic of late Victorian book titles. Roughtor is reached easily from Camelford, and down by the ford at the moorland edge a lonely granite memorial marks the scene of a tragedy where a servant girl was murdered by her lover Matthew Weeks in 1844. The latter's trial and subsequent hanging at Bodmin caught the public imagination. Charles Causley's poem 'The Ballad of Charlotte Dymond' tells the tale.

Blisland was Norden's "parishe standinge nere the Moares and craggie hills." Margaret Leigh's *Harvest of the Moor* (1937) described the moor and farming here at Newton ('Trenoweth'). The village itself was a favourite of John

Betjeman, who considered its church to be "the first really beautiful work of man which my boyhood vividly remembers...it looks over the tree tops of a deep and elmy valley and away to the west where, like a silver shield, the Atlantic shines..." ('Blisland', 1948). He never forgot his first visit, when he cycled inland from Trebetherick by the sea.

Altarnun Church

ALTARNUN

The mysterious vicar of Altarnun, Francis Davey, was the villain behind the story of *Jamaica Inn*, and it was to him that Mary Yelland erroneously came for help. Charles Causley's poem 'A Short Life of Nevil Northey Burnard' celebrates the Cornish sculptor who was born in 1818 at Altarnun, where he "broke syllables of light from the moorstone" which lay hereabouts. He became famous, but died in poverty sixty years later at Redruth Workhouse. Wesley's bust on the old chapel at Altarnun is one of his carvings. By coincidence, the Wesley cottage is just up the road at Trewint.

Wesley House at Trewint 'About two we came to Trewint [Diggory Isbell's house], wet and weary enough, having been battered by the rain and hail for some hours.' (John Wesley, *Journal*, 2nd April 1744)

The Charlotte Dymond Memorial at Roughtor Ford. "Charlotte went from our house And never came home again." (Charles Causley, 'The Ballad of Charlotte Dymond')

LAUNCESTON

Launceston is the town of the poet Charles Causley. Several of his poems are of Launceston or the surrounding area. The magnificent granite carvings which face St Mary Magdalene's church include the reclining figure of the saint which inspired Causley's poem 'Mary, Mary Magdelene'. 'A True Ballad of Sir Henry Trecarrel' tells of the financing of the church by the lord of nearby Trecarrel manor. Causley's poem 'Homecoming' is of course to Launceston. By coincidence, A. L. Rowse's 'Home-Coming to Cornwall: December 1942' was in a wartime train diverted through "Launceston perched on a shoulder like Liege," and then onward into north Cornwall. Thomas Hardy called Launceston 'St Kerrs' when *A Pair of Blue Eyes* was published in 1873, but he changed it to 'St Launce's' in 1895. It was "the market town and station nearest to Endelstow." The station was on the broad gauge line from Plymouth via Tavistock, opened in 1865. Hardy must have anticipated the new station at 'Camelton' (Camelford), on the extension of the North Cornwall Railway (London & South Western Railway from Exeter) through Launceston (1886) and Camelford (1893). Hardy's 'Falcon Inn' is the White Hart Hotel in Broad Street.

Church wall carving, Launceston
"Mary, Mary Magdalene
Lying on the wall.."
(Charles Causley, 'Mary, Mary Magdalene')

Launceston "Castle and keep, uprearing gray..."
(Thomas Hardy, 'St Launce's Revisted')

BODMIN AND THE CUCKOO RAILWAY

'Q' was born in November 1863 at Bodmin (his 'Tregarrick'), where his father Thomas practised as a doctor. There is a small memorial to him opposite the parish church. His short story *Cuckoo Valley Railway* describes the Bodmin & Wadebridge Railway down the 'Cuckoo' (Camel) valley, from "the slope of a high and sombre moorland" to 'Ponteglos' (Wadebridge). 'Dunford Bridge' is Wenfordbridge, the terminus where a train of eight trucks waited. 'Q' rode on the engine "with a prodigiously long funnel, bearing the name The Wonder of the Age," while two newly-weds rode in the one empty truck. "Far down on our right, the river shone between the trees, and these trees, encroaching on the track, almost joined their branches above us. Ahead, the moss that grew upon the sleepers gave the line the appearance of a green glade, and the grasses, starred with golden-rod and mallow, grew tall to the very edge of the rails." At the Dunmere level-crossing (where the A389 Wadebridge road descends from Bodmin), they met a christening party, so the driver, stoker and all partook of the cake. Alas, the final clay train used this wonderfully scenic line in 1983 and the rails were lifted soon after. Its course is now a path and cycleway, which can be followed all the way down to Wadebridge and Padstow.

St Enodoc Church and Bray Hill

PETROC'S COAST

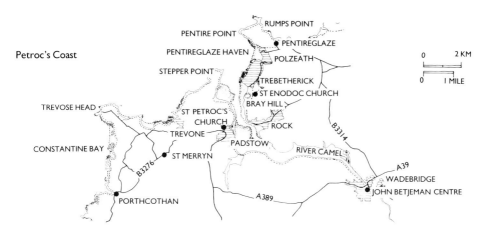

Petroc's Coast

This is the north coast on either side of the Camel estuary, the landing place of the Celtic saint Petroc, with important church dedications at Padstow and upstream at Bodmin.

"...Here Petroc landed, here I stand today
The same Atlantic surges roll for me
As rolled for Parson Hawker..."

wrote Sir John Betjeman in his poem 'North Coast Recollections'. Betjeman is the most famous literary name to be associated with this area. He came to stay during his childhood at his father's house Undertown at Trebetherick (Daymer Bay), and returned frequently in later years to his own house, Treen. His great love for Cornwall is seen in his poetry and other writing. The poem 'Trebetherick' recalls childhood picnics on the clifftops, and looking for wreckage

"... when a storm was at its height,
And feathery slate was black in rain...
...Waves full of treasure then were roaring up the beach."

His longer 'North Coast Recollections' returns all the time to the atmosphere of the coastline, the golden sand of the bar at low tide, while "...Stepper-wards, the sun
Sends Bray Hill's phantoms
stretching to the church."

The church of the poem is the dune-surrounded St Enodoc, where Betjeman's slate tombstone has become a place of pilgrimage since he was buried here in sight of the sea in 1984. He has a different memorial at the head of the estuary, where the old Wadebridge railway station has been converted to the John Betjeman Centre. It contains an exhibition of memorabilia.

The John Betjeman Centre in the old railway station at Wadebridge.

Down the estuary, and almost opposite Trebetherick, Padstow is the birthplace and home of Donald Rawe, a writer, poet and dramatist with Cornwall very much at heart. Across on the Atlantic coast, D. H. and Frieda Lawrence stayed at J. D. Beresford's cottage at Porthcothan from December 1915 until they moved to Zennor in March 1916.

Baring-Gould wrote of the coast on either side of the estuary. *In the Roar of the Sea* is a dramatic tale of wrecking and smuggling set around Pentireglaze and Polzeath. Judith Trevisa, daughter of the rector of St Enodoc church, is married to Cruel Coppinger, a name taken from the legendary villain described further up the coast by Hawker. The less popular *The Gaverocks* begins in the parish of 'St Kevin' (St Merryn) around 'Nantsillan Cove,' a "horseshoe bay gnawed by the Atlantic surge out of the rocky coast" lying between 'Sillan

Point' and 'Cardue Head.' This would seem to be around Constantine Bay (Hender Gaverock's younger son is called Constantine), but the author took elements from many parts of the coast on either side of Trevose Head.

ARTHUR'S SHORE

TINTAGEL

Tintagel Castle is the birthplace of King Arthur according to Geoffrey of Monmouth. Its romantic ruins on the Island and mainland are separated by a narrow neck, the crossing of which Norden described "as may astonish an unstable brayne to consider the perill, for the leaste slipp of the foote sendes the whole bodye into the devouring sea..."

The literary world of the nineteenth century put Tintagel firmly on the map. Tennyson is perhaps the most famous name here, but he was certainly not the only writer to visit the place. An early admirer was the Rev Richard Warner, whose *A Tour Through Cornwall in the Autumn of 1808* states it "conjured up all the visions of its ancient magnificent." R. S. Hawker honeymooned here in 1823 and 'The Quest of

the Sangraal' followed later, describing "grim Dundagel throned along the sea." His poem 'The Wreck' pictured

".... dark Cornwall's rifted shore,
Old Arthur's stern and rugged keep:
There, where proud billows dash and roar,
His haughty turret guards the deep."

Tennyson produced his 'Morte d'Arthur' in 1842, and when the first four 'Idylls of the King' were published in 1859, he was encouraged to write more of the epic. So he toured Cornwall and the Scillies in 1860, mostly in the company of Francis Palgrave. He recorded at Tintagel: "grand coast, furious rain...Black cliffs and caves and storm and wind, but I weather it out and

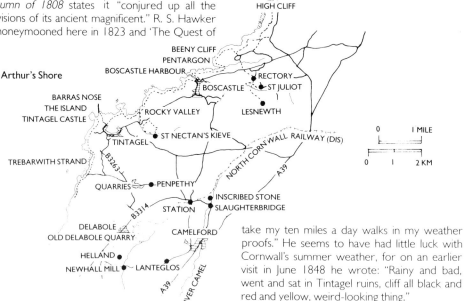

Arthur's Shore

take my ten miles a day walks in my weather proofs." He seems to have had little luck with Cornwall's summer weather, for on an earlier visit in June 1848 he wrote: "Rainy and bad, went and sat in Tintagel ruins, cliff all black and red and yellow, weird-looking thing."

Charles Dickens and Wilkie Collins passed through Tintagel on their Cornish tours, but the

Tintagel Castle "Tintagil castle by the Cornish sea." (Tennyson, 'The Coming of Arthur')

poet Algernon Swinburne lodged with the painter J. W. Inchbold at the village schoolhouse in 1864. He got involved, physically, in the Atlantic and rugged coastline when he cut a foot badly while swimming and exploring caves and was laid up for three weeks. He described "the double ruin, one half facing the other, of the old castle or palace of the kings of Cornwall," and his 'Tristram of Lyonesse' was conceived here.

Francis Kilvert's party spent a few hours at Tintagel on 3rd August 1870. Guided by the daughter of the custodian, they first viewed the castle and examined the cove where Merlin found the boy Arthur in Tennyson's 'Idylls'. Then they bought photographs and loitered back to the inn through the "dreadful heat" to the inn for dinner — a visit with the hallmarks of the true tourist!

Thomas Hardy visited the castle at about the same time when courting Emma Gifford, and they got locked in. Emma knew the district well and her unpublished novel *The Maid on the Shore* was set at Tintagel. Hardy later used the castle's Great Hall as the setting for his one-act play *The Famous Tragedy of the Queen of Cornwall*, another working of the Tristram and Iseult story. With the play he published an imaginary sketch of the castle.

The village at Tintagel was named Trevena until its growing popularity brought about a change of name at the end of the nineteenth century. More tourists came after the North Cornwall Railway was opened to Camelford in 1893, and the massive King Arthur's Castle Hotel was soon built. To preserve the headland of Barras Nose from further development, the young National Trust made its first coastal purchase in 1897 as a memorial to Tennyson.

Tintagel's church is perched on an ancient site above high cliffs overlooking the castle. "Black with rain and time and storm," Swinburne called it. A stained glass window is dedicated to John

Douglas Cook, who was buried in the churchyard in 1868. He edited the *Morning Chronicle* and was a founder-editor of the *Saturday Review*. In *Some Recollections*, Emma Hardy recalled him in the 1860s as "a great and important visitor" who came to the village every summer. He built Trevena House, now the front of the Hall of Chivalry and King Arthur's Hall which Frederick Glasscock added after the Great War.

SLATE COUNTRY

Trebarwith Strand (Hardy's 'Barwith Strand') is along the coast 1½ miles south of Tintagel Castle. The valley inland from here is scarred with slate quarries, still like Kilvert's description of "a wild strange country, the road passing between high cliffs and bastions of slate in piles, or stone banks supporting the sides of the slate quarries." Hardy's poem 'Green Slates' reflects on a visit to a quarry here at Penpethy to select roofing slates in 1870. In *Old Delabole* (1915), Eden Phillpotts described how Edith Retallack sat on the cliffs at Trebarwith contemplating the sea breaking on the shore. However, most of the book was set inland at Delabole, where the great quarry and all its workings around the turn of the century were described in detail. Down in the valley below the quarry is Newhall Mill where Edith's betrothed, Wesley Bake, was the miller. Celia Fiennes, who visited 'Bole' in the 1690s, was just one of many travellers to have described the famous old quarry.

Two miles east, Camelford was the birthplace of J. ,D. Cook. Tennyson came here twice to

Wilberforce Retallack's home in Delabole Quarry. "...beside the trees on the knoll, stands a whitewashed cottage, high above the bottom of the quarries, but far below their surface..." (Eden Phillpotts, *Old Delabole*)

visit the inscribed stone by the River Camel at Slaughterbridge where legend has it Arthur hid or meditated after his last fatal battle. The inscription 'Latini (hic iacit filius Macari' translates as 'Latinus lies here the son of Macarus'. Palgrave recorded the second occasion: "It lay below the bank; and in his eagerness to reach it and sit down, Arthur's poet slipped right into the stream, and returned laughing to Camelford."

GLEN NECTAN AND THE SILENT TOWER

Between Tintagel and Boscastle is the attractive St Nectan's or St Knighton's Kieve with a waterfall. A traditional meeting place of the Knights of the Round Table, the Kieve was also popular with writers and artists. It was on the itineraries of Dickens, Collins, Mrs Craik (in 1867 and 1883) and many others. Maclise painted 'A Girl at a Waterfall' after his visit with Dickens in 1842. The latter bought it by a "pious fraud" through a third party, to prevent Maclise giving it to him or selling it too cheaply! Hawker's poem 'The Sisters of Glen Nectan' is the sad tale of two old ladies who lived in a cottage by the waterfall. Victorian novels which used this romantic spot include Miss Braddon's *Mount Royal*, Rev G.MacDonald's *A Seaboard Parish* and Rev F. Talbot O'Donaghue's *St Knighton's Keive*. The stream follows the Rocky Valley down to the coast, where Anthony Trollope's story *Malachi's Cove* was located further back towards Tintagel.

Forrabury church stands on the edge of ancient fields outside Boscastle, just before the coast road descends to the little harbour. Hawker's poem 'The Silent Tower of Bottreaux' refers to the sinking of a ship while bringing bells for the church. The pilot thanked God when they heard the guiding bells of Tintagel, but the master blastphemed and a storm arose, wrecking the ship outside Boscastle, so

"still when the storm of Bottreaux' waves
Is wakening in his weedy caves:
Those bells, that sullen surges hide,
Peal their deep notes beneath the tide."

Thus the bells are said to announce a coming storm, just as the church bells of Lyonesse are also heard beneath the waves.

HARDY COUNTRY

The district around Boscastle and its dramatic coastline made a great impression on Thomas Hardy, who called it a place "pre-eminently (for one person at least) the region of dream and mystery. The ghostly birds, the pall-like sea, the frothy wind, the eternal soliloquy of the waters, the bloom of dark purple cast that seems to exhale from the shoreward precipices, in themselves lend to the scene an atmosphere like the twilight of a night vision."

Hardy first came in March 1870 to make plans of St Juliot's church and later supervise its restoration. Here at the rectory he met his first wife Emma Lavinia Gifford, who was sister-in-law of the Rev Caddell Holder. *A Pair of Blue Eyes* recalls these events, in which a trainee architect Stephen Smith arrives to measure the church at 'West Endelstow' (St Juliot) for restoration and meets Elfride Swancourt, the vicar's daughter. There is great drama when Henry Knight demonstrates the backward eddy of the wind on the 'Cliff Without a Name' (identified variously as Beeny Cliff or High Cliff). He slips and nearly

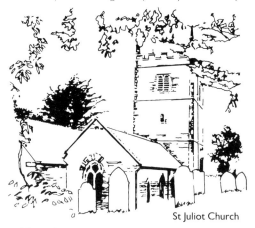

St Juliot Church

falls to his death, but is saved by Elfride. Meanwhile, his rival Smith passes by unaware on the steamer *Puffin* bound from Bristol for Boscastle. Elfride finally marries the recently widowed Lord Luxellian of 'Endelstow House' only to die five months later of a miscarriage. The house at 'East Endelstow' (Lesnewth) is based on Lanhydrock House near Bodmin, with elements of Athelhampton Hall back in Hardy's Dorset.

Boscastle Harbour, Thomas Hardy's 'Castle Boterel'

Hardy first called Boscastle 'Stranton' when his novel was first published in 1873, but he re-named it 'Castle Boterel' in a revision of 1895. With the use of a map, a circular 'Hardy walk' of about 4 miles can be devised from here, taking in the Valency valley, St Juliot church, rectory and the cliffs. Other writers have observed Boscastle's astonishing harbour, so narrow and dominated by steep cliffs. Walter White likened it to Balaclava when he came here at the time of the Crimean War, a description repeated in later guidebooks. Swinburne rode here at night in September 1864, finding "very queer, dark grey swollen water, caught as it were in a trap, and heaving with rage against both sides at once..." Victorian novelists used the location, for example the story of T. Mullett Ellis's *The Beauty of Boscastle: A Melodramatic and Psychological Story* (1893) travels from Boscastle to Monte Carlo, Venice, Switzerland and back. Baring-Gould's *John Herring* (1883) is mainly of Devon but has Boscastle harbour in it.

St Juliot's church stands on a slope a little distance from the rectory and is reached only by lanes or a footpath up from the Valency valley. There are wall memorials to Hardy and Holder, and one which Hardy had erected after Emma died in 1912. He wrote the poem 'The Marble Tablet' upon seeing it in September 1916 when he returned to the scene of their courtship. After Emma's death, he expressed his thoughts in some of his best love poetry.

Hardy revisited the coast and Beeny Cliff, where "Still in all its chasmal beauty bulks old Beeny to the sky." 'After a Journey', written at Pentargon Bay, sees him led back by Emma's ghost to view the cliffs, cave and waterfall where they walked together when they first met. The couple also walked in the Valency valley, where 'Under the Waterfall' recalls a picnic in August 1870 beside
"... the purl of a little valley fall
About three spans wide and two spans tall."
The fall is thought to be just above the foot-bridge crossing to Minster church. They lost a small drinking glass while rinsing it here, so
"There lies intact that chalice of ours,
And its presence adds to the rhyme of love
Persistently sung by the fall above.
No lip has touched it since his and mine
In turns there from sipped lovers' wine."

Beeny Cliff "Still in all its chasmal beauty bulks old Beeny to the sky." (Thomas Hardy, 'Beeny Cliff')

HAWKER COUNTRY

This windswept district beyond Bude in the remote north of Cornwall was described concisely by Charles Kingsley as "the Coombes of the Far West...which cut the high table-land of the confines of Devon and Cornwall...Each has its upright walls, inland of rich oak-wood, nearer the sea of dark-green furze, then of smooth turf, then of weird black cliffs which range out right and left far into the deep sea, in castles, spires and wings of jagged ironstone...Each has its black field of jagged shark's-tooth rock which paves the cove from side to side...laced with white foam from the eternal surge, stretching in parallel lines out to the westward, in strata set upright on edge, or tilted towards each other at strange angles by primeval earthquakes. Such is the 'Mouth', as these coves are called; and such the jaw of teeth which they display, one rasp of which would grind abroad the timbers of the stoutest ship. To landward, all richness, softness, and peace; to seaward, a waste and howling wilderness of rock and roller, barren to the fishermen, and hopeless to the shipwrecked mariner." (*Westward Ho!*)

Morwenstow is best known for the poet Robert Stephen Hawker, who was vicar of this "sea-washed parish" in 1834-75. His church stands in view of the sea but partly sheltered in a coombe. Hawker of Morwenstow will be remembered for more than his eccentricities, such as dressing in a fisherman's jersey and waders. He introduced the Harvest Festival in 1843, and gave Christian burials to sailors shipwrecked along the fearsome 'iron bound coast.' Around forty sailors are buried in the churchyard, once marked by the keels of upturned boats, now by a granite cross inscribed 'Unknown yet Well Known.' The white figurehead of the Scottish brig *Caledonia* stands above her captain. She was wrecked near Higher Sharpnose Point in September 1842 when homeward bound from Odessa, leaving one survivor. Hawker described the wreck in 'The Remembrances of a Cornish Vicar' in *Footprints of Former Men in Far Cornwall*.

Inside the church is a stained glass window unveiled to Hawker's memory in 1904, depicting various aspects such as the figurehead of the *Caledonia*, Hawker and his dog, and St Morwenna's well. At the foot of the pulpit is Char-

lotte Hawker's tomb of 1863 (although a space was left for him, Hawker was buried at Plymouth). Charlotte was twice his age when they married in 1823. Hawker remarried in 1864 and this time his second wife, Pauline, was 20 while he was 61! An eccentric to the last, he was received into the Roman Catholic Church hours before his death in Plymouth in 1875.

Morwenstow Church stands in sight of the iron-bound coast of north Cornwall

Hawker's vicarage can be seen below the churchyard. Its unusual chimneys represent the towers of churches with which he was connected. Down on Vicarage Cliff, Hawker's Hut was built of wood from shipwrecks. Here he watched for ships in distress, meditated and composed verses. 'The Storm', however, was "written on a rock by the shore." To the north, the Gull Rock off Marsland Mouth was the scene of the final departure of the mysterious pirate, smuggler and wrecker Cruel Coppinger who plagued this wild coast, described in Hawker's *Footprints*. It was Marsland Mouth from which the Jesuits escaped by boat after being chased by Amyas Leigh and Will Cary in *Westward Ho!* The poet and playwright Ronald Duncan made his home in the Marsland valley, right on the Cornwall-Devon border.

Elizabeth Godfrey took this borderland for her *Cornish Diamonds*. The cliffs feature when Denis Kay walks from 'Gooseburn Mill' (Gooseham Mill) along the shore to 'Kerranstow' (Morwenstow). He climbs the dangerous cliffs at 'Shag's Head' (Vicarage Cliff?), becomes stuck and falls, but is rescued by rope when Jenifer Lyon sees him and gets help. This can be compared with Thomas Hardy's incident at Beeny Cliff near Boscastle. The book concludes happily when Jenifer encounters Captain Alick Studland at the stile to the cliffs from 'Kerranstow' churchyard, complete with its figurehead, although of a Norse ship.

Kingsley wrote part of *Westward Ho!* over the Tidna valley from Morwenstow at Tonacombe Manor. This was 'Chapel' in the book. The cottage of Rose Salterne (the 'Rose of Torridge') was in the Coombe valley below Stowe Barton. The Grenville's Old Stowe House is no more, and nor is New Stowe House except for the stables converted to a farm house. From the garden, Amyas Leigh and Sir Richard Grenville could glimpse the Atlantic and inland to "the lofty tower of Kilkhampton Church, rich with the monuments and offerings of five centuries of Grenvilles." Hawker claimed to have composed 'The Song of the Western Men' "under a stag-horned oak in Sir Beville's Walk in Stowe Wood."

The heroic sea captain Sir Richard Grenville was immortalised in the ballad 'The Revenge', perhaps inspired when Tennyson visited this area. A later Sir Richard was courting Honor Harris when she was crippled in a riding accident at Stowe in Daphne du Maurier's *The Kings General*. In 1643, the Royalist Sir Bevil Grenville was victor at the Battle of Stamford Hill at Stratton. 'Q' used this battle in *The Silver Spur*, when Jack Marvel fought here and later rescued Delia Killigrew as she was landed from a small boat on the nearby coast, perhaps at Northcott Mouth. This is just north of Bude, a place visited by Tennyson and Hardy, the latter calling it "Stratleigh, a small watering place."

Hawker's rectory at Morwenstow

SELECTED FURTHER READING

By necessity this is a very short list. Some publishers have reprinted earlier classics in recent years (such as Alison Hodge of Penzance, Tabb House of Padstow or Anthony Mott's Cornish Library series), but for many of the earlier or rarer titles described in the text, the interested reader will be required to visit a good Cornish library or secondhand bookshop.

Betjeman, J. *Betjeman's Cornwall* (Murray, 1984)
Blight, J. T. *A Week at the Land's End* (1861; reprinted Alison Hodge, 1989)
Du Maurier, D. *Enchanted Cornwall* (Guild Publishing, 1989)
Ellis, P. B. *The Cornish Language and its Literature* (Routledge & Kegan Paul, 1974)
Graham, W. *Poldark's Cornwall* (Bodley Head, 1983)
Kilvert, F. *Kilvert's Cornish Diary* (ed. by R. Maber and A. Tregoning; Alison Hodge, 1989)
Padel, O. J. *A Popular Dictionary of Cornish Place-Names* (Alison Hodge, 1988)
Phelps, K. *The Wormwood Cup: Thomas Hardy in Cornwall* (Lodenek Press, 1975)
Rowse, A. L. *Quiller-Couch: A Portrait of Q* (Methuen, 1988)
Rowse, A. L. (ed.) *Cornish Anthology* (Alison Hodge, 1990)
Thomas, D. M. (ed) *The Granite Kingdom: Poems of Cornwall* (Bradford Barton, 1970)
Val Baker, D. *The Spirit of Cornwall* (1980)
Val Baker, D. *The Timeless Land: the Creative Spirit in Cornwall* (Adams & Dart, 1973)
Val Baker, D. (ed) *Cornish Short Stories* (Penguin 1976)
Williams, M. (ed) *My Cornwall* (Bossiney Books, 1973)

Special thanks are given to Terry Knight and the staff of the Cornish Studies Library, Redruth.

John Betjeman's slate gravestone, St Enodoc churchyard.

Front cover: Q Memorial and Fowey Harbour

ISBN 0 906294 26 6   ©   Peter Stanier   1992
First published 1992 by Twelveheads Press, Chy Mengleth, Twelveheads, Truro, Cornwall TR4 8SN.